# MODERN DANCE TERMINOLOGY

## PAUL LOVE

*With a New Introduction*

*by Eleanor King*

*A REPUBLICATION BY DANCE HORIZONS*

A DANCE HORIZONS BOOK
Princeton Book Company, Publishers


ISBN 0-87127-206-7
Library of Congress Catalog Card Number 96-71976
Printed in the United States of America

# INTRODUCTION

Paul Love, artist and critic, with keen insight collected and helped to define the terminology which appeared with the emergence and establishment of modern dance. First published in 1953, *Modern Dance Terminology* provides an encyclopedic view of the aims, theories and objectives of the pioneer artists, shedding light on their achieved revolution.

Quotations from the deathless *Art Of The Dance* (by Isadora Duncan) lead all the rest, with eighteen references; *New York Times* dance critic and writer John Martin has six entries; other art and music critics are cited and direct quotations from Dalcroze, Laban, Wigman, Holm, Humphrey, St. Denis, Weidman, Graham, Limón, Nikolais, Tamiris and Tetley give authenticity to this nomenclature.

The new dance discovered and applied such vital principles as Humphrey's fall and recovery and Graham's tension and release.

Paul Love predicted an eventual fusion of modern dance and ballet; it proceeds, but slowly. In the last few decades, modern dancers have exercised at the ballet barre. Conversely, several world ballet companies have included, among others, *The Moor's Pavane*, that modern dance classic, in their repertory. We admired Nureyev for essaying the role of Othello, but the essential quality of *gravitas*, the weight of the original Limón creation, always eluded him as this quality was not a part of ballet discipline. It will require many more decades before the classic school integrates such diametrically opposed principles. While ballet technique works from outside-in, modern works from inside-out.

There is no doubt that modern dance will continue to be the seed of the future. Paul Love also predicted that early works would form the repertoire of new companies—and that is increasingly true. Choreography with content is now respectfully sought. Such works give to ranks of new dancers a sense of belonging to and continuing a great tradition.

The understanding of the seminal works and techniques requires more than superficial study, pointing to the importance of this reprint of *Modern Dance Terminology*.

*Eleanor King*
*Santa Fe*

ABA FORM. One of the simplest compositional forms used by the modern dance, wherein two movement-themes are presented successively and are followed by a repetition of the first theme, with or without variations. The duration of each theme is subject to the wishes of the choreographer. The ABA form is widely used in music. It is synonymous with folk form; see also song-form.

ABSOLUTE DANCE. The term originated in Germany as a result of the emphasis on dynamic form in the German dance during the 1920's and 1930's. It denotes a dance built on movement alone, without assistance from music or the other arts. In this sense, it is analogous to the tendency toward pure form in the other arts during the same period. It does not signify the ultimate or perfect dance, as has sometimes been stated.

The results of experiments in the so-called absolute dance were a full knowledge of physical as distinguished from musical rhythms; of the ebb and flow of muscular impulse; relaxation and tension; and of movement as the substance of the dance. Absolute dance is thus synonymous with the term modern dance, which is less limited in meaning. Absolute dance is rarely presented in its purest sense at the present, since the discoveries enabled choreographers to add music and setting while still keeping movement dominant.

The term absolute dance was one effort on the part of dancers to distinguish the new type of dance from the classical ballet. In addition to being confused with the term modern dance, it has also been considered synonymous with abtract dance. It may be partially so considered in that it usually conveys an emotional mood rather than a concrete subject. However, it is invariably without music, whereas abstract dance may or may not use musical accompaniment. "The term is inaccurate," John Martin contends, "for there is nothing at all in the nature or the purpose of this kind of dancing which prevents it from being programmatic if it chooses. It has never confined itself, even in its most experimental period, to absoluteness. Indeed, it could not do so from its very nature, for the movement of the human body is inevitably associated with experience and cannot be made into an abstraction of line and form under any circumstances." Note 1.

It was originally conceived as synonymous with dance without music but is only partially so, since the latter may be an expression of an emotion, idea, or mood, and therefore also absolute dance, or an expression of a concrete subject, and therefore also dramatic or programmatic dance.

It has also been called expressionistic dance by the German dancer, Mary Wigman, and her followers. The term should be discarded for the same reason that abstract dance should be discarded.

ABSTRACT DANCE. It is that type of dance which works in abstract movement to build a mood or convey an idea. It has been discriminately applied to all types of modern dance not immediately understood by the critic or spectator. Inasmuch as the movements of the body cannot be made into a pure abstraction of line and form and still convey any meaning, it would seem expedient to avoid the term. Abstract dance at one time referred only to a dance whose main medium was bodily movement: movements and movement-phrases originated, ordered, developed, repeated, contrasted, etc., in order to convey moods or ideas. This movement was removed in varying degrees from the naturalistic or literal; but, becaue the human body was the instrument, it could not achieve that reduction to pure line and area which was possible in non-objective painting.

The American dancer, Helen Tamiris, has suggested the term thematic dance to replace abstract dance.

Abstract dance at present includes all dances which are not restricted by story or plot. It would thus include Doris Humphrey's New Dance, Martha Graham's highly evocative Frontier, Ruth St. Denis's visualization of Schubert's Unfinished Symphony, George Balanchine's Concerto Barocco, Michel Fokine's Les Sylphides, and Oscar Schlemmer's Triadic Ballet. The movement in Graham's Frontier is close to kinetic pantomime; the movement in Schlemmer's Triadic Ballet is totally subservient to the abstract costumes which it conveys around the stage like chessmen. By including such diverse dances as these, the term abstract dance has ceased to have any meaning.

ABSTRACT MOVEMENT. That movement which, for expressive purposes, is greatest removed from natural everyday movement. The term is usually applied to movement used for the expression of moods, ideas, concepts, etc., in contradistinction to dramatic, natural, or pantomimic movement used for the expression of specific subjects, situations, etc. It is movement that is "considered apart from any application to a particular object," or "that which comprises or concentrates in itself the essential qualities of a larger thing or of several things." Note 2.

Movement is regarded as abstract in modern dance when it is a precipitation or discovering and drawing apart of the essence of the subject for emphasis; it is not used in modern dance in the sense of vagueness or the removal from life into a bloodless geometry. In general, it may refer to all movement used for an art-form, since such is usually always withdrawn, separated, epitomized, summarized, and abridged. However, for convenience and clarity, the degree of abridgement must be taken into consideration. Thus, abstract movement denotes the greatest degree of abridgement and removal. The smallest degree of abstraction, i.e., that which remains closest to the natural, is commonly called pantomimic or natural movement.

Movement should never reach complete abstraction; indeed, in its very nature, it is incapable of doing so. "Any theory of dance that attempts to make use of the body as an instrument of pure design is doomed to failure, for the body is of all possible instruments the least removable from the associations of experience. There is no movement of any of its members that can conceivably be separated from implications of usefulness, whether they are positive or negative implications." Note 3.

See also ABSTRACT DANCE, ABSOLUTE DANCE.

ACCELERANDO. An acceleration or increase in time, as distinguished from crescendo, which is an increase in force.

Antonyms: RALLENTANDO, RITARDANDO.

ACCENT. A stronger or sharper movement in a series of movements, the chief element being force. Accents may be given to one or more parts of a movment-phrase, or to a number of movement-phrases in relation to other phrases.

Synonym: STRESS.

ACCUMULATIVE RHYTHM. See CUMULATIVE FORM.

ACTION-MODE. As "steps" is used for the ballet, "action-modes" may be used for the modern dance. The term was suggested by Elizabeth Selden but has never come into general usage. Such a term was felt necessary to describe movement in the modern dance where the whole body is involved in the movement and where the distinction between foot-work and arm-work is not so sharply indicated as it is in the ballet.

A better term would appear to be movement-phrase.

ACTIVE MOVEMENT. That movement which is impelled by will-power and conscious driving force, as distinguished from passive movement which seems to be impelled by its own momentum.

AESTHETIC DANCING. Originally denoted a much simplified and weakened form of ballet; also used to describe any type of dance not unaesthetic. Such dancing is usually tepid, sentimental, pretty, and without idea or serious expression. The term should be discarded.

AMERICAN DANCE. It has been suggested elsewhere (see German dance, space) that the German dance, despite its revolutionary technique, was an expression of the emotional individual and thus a continuation, if one will not accept culmination, of western culture. The German dynamic principle of tension-relaxation refers to varying degrees of muscular activity; it ranges from all to none. Relaxation, it should be noted, follows tension and infers a type of movement that is constantly waning or lessening. The American dynamic principles, contraction-release and fall-recovery, are both affirmative; their accent is on the active movement. Furthermore, they are not degrees of muscular activity but kinds of movement. It is this more positive character that leads one to believe that the American dance may extend itself into the future. The technique of both the German and the American dance has been based upon natural rhythms and natural movements. The German, however, has been directed toward an expression of the past. The application of the American has been in a different direction. The German has been snuffed out; the American still lives. It is too early to predict its development, except to utter a hope that it may be the seed of the future.

ANGULAR MOVEMENT. A type of movement accenting straight lines and angles; used in modern dance in contradistinction to curved movement. Angular movement is percussive and broken; it takes interruptions and is staccato and not legato.

See also PERCUSSIVE MOVEMENT.

ANNSPANNUNG-ABSPANNUNG. A German term referring to the ebb and flow of muscular impulses.

See TENSION-RELAXATION.

APPLIED DANCE. Term suggested by Elizabeth Selden to denote dance in the service of other arts such as theater, opera, etc., where the drama or music are the dominants, subjecting movement to their own peculiar necessities. An unnecessary term.

ARCHITECTURAL. An adjective sometimes applied to the modern dance because of its use of self-evolutionary or sequential movement, each movement depending upon the preceding one and containing the birth of the succeeding one; because of the inability of any movement or phrase, the building block, to be removed without causing a complete redistribution or collapse of all other parts; because of its use of volume, mass, and space in predominance over line and plane; and because the structure of a modern dance is never complete until the last movement has been performed. In this sense, a modern dance, using movement as its material, builds from its opening to its closing movement, its complete structure never being presented until the curtain falls.

ART-DANCE. The term originated in the early stages of the modern dance and was used to denote a "dance with a purpose," or "serious dancing," as opposed to dance for entertainment. It was never commonly used in America but has been accepted in Germany in literature of the so-called Free Dance. The term is vague and pretentious.

See MODERN DANCE.

AXIAL MOVEMENT. Movement around an axis, such as arm movements around the individual body as an axis, or the movement of one group around another group as an axis. The German-American dancer, Hanya Holm, divides axial movement into two phases, resting axis and turning axis. Movement around a resting axis may be illustrated by arm movements around a stationary torso, or the movements of several dancers around a stationary dancer, etc. Movement around a turning axis may be illustrated by arm movement around a turning body, etc.

Axial movement is movement around one or more axes in the body, whereas locomotor movement is movement from place to place. Axial movement may, however, also occur in a body progressing in space and therefore the distinction from locomotor movement is not absolute. Generally, axial movement occurs without progression in space. Swinging, turning, and beating movements are illustrations of axial movement.

BALANCE. A constant redistribution of body members so that the body remains in equipoise. For the dancer, balance is a consciously produced synthesis of physical and mental energies whose purpose is to achieve a dynamic balance instead of the static state implied in the common usage of the word. The impulse to movement and the intensity of the movement must be controlled. Balance, therefore, may be called a result of the harmonious relation of impulse, energy, and intensity. Hanya Holm.

BALANCE-UNBALANCE. The term is synonymous with and should be replaced by fall-recovery.

BALLET. A composition of dances expressing a poetic idea or a dramatic story with connecting pantomimic action, costumes, scenery, and accompanying music. The term ballet has been so long associated with classic theatrical dancing that it has come to mean also the type of steps, postures, attitudes, and movements that were developed during the history of classic theatrical dancing. Because of this, it leads to confusion when applied to a dance or series of dances using modern technique. When so applied, it should be prefaced by the word "modern" to distinguish the dance from classic ballet, symphonic ballet, etc.

See also CONCERT DANCE, GROUP DANCE.

BALLISTIC SWING. Distinguished from a pendular swing through the fact that energy is visibly applied to the swinging member so that the path of the curve and its termination are sharply marked. Ballistic refers to the ballista, an ancient machine used for throwing heavy objects, which in its turn is derived from the Greek word, ballein, to throw. The ballistic swing is forcibly projected and does not depend upon the pull of gravity implied in the pendulum in order to provide its back and forth motion. The diminishing arcs that may occur in the pendular swing are never present in the ballistic swing.

BAREFOOT DANCING. Any dance which stresses the freedom of the bare foot as distinguished from the restriction of the ballet slipper; equivalent to the term toe dancing in ballet, and as undescriptive.

It was Isadora Duncan's rejection of the ballet slipper that led to a barefoot dancing craze that reached its height probably between 1906 and 1911.

BASIC DANCE. An inclusive term that attempts to denote the similar·ities rather than the differences between dance forms. "At the root of all these varied manifestations of dancing, and of countless other manifestations, as well, lies the common impulse to resort to movement to externalize emotional states which we cannot externalize by rational means. This is basic dance." Note 4. "Its stuff is the creative movement evolved from the dancer's spontaneous awareness of his relation to his environment; its subject matter ranges throughout the field of extra-intellectual experience; its form is the creative shaping of the material according to its own dictates in the interest of intelligibility; its music is inherently the vocal complement of its movement; its method of communication is a purely kinesthetic one." Note 5.

BEATING. Quick movements back and forth that are greatly limited in range. They differ from shaking movements only in that they are directed against some resistance, actual or imaginary. Because of this, the tension is likely to be greater in beating than in shaking movements, although there may be many exceptions to this. In both, the impelling energy is maintained throughout the movement, ie., the movement is stopped before the energy dissipates itself.

BODY-CONTROL. The purpose of all elementary exercises in any modern dance technique; these are so arranged as to make the beginning dancer aware of his body as an integer and able to control it so that no parts are inactive or dead, whether moving or not. Such exercises are the preparation for more difficult problems in balance, extension, etc.

BODY CORRECTIVES. A series of exercises designed to alleviate and correct certain physical deficiencies and defects. The so-called health dance and natural dance are for hygienic purposes rather than for specific corrections.

BREATH IMPULSE. "That impulse toward movement which is determined by the breath rhythm of the body. Such an impulse has been generally used as a basis for a dance technic by dancers trained in the methods of the German modern dance." Gertrude Lippincott

BREATH RHYTHM. 1. One of the natural physical rhythms which was observed and consciously used by followers of Isadora Duncan and others. The use of these natural rhythms was later formulated under the term dynamism. The inhalation and expiration of the breath, taken as a synthesis, provide a natural physical rhythm and may be used as a dynamic governing principle, the various lengths and exaggerations providing a dynamic rhythm.

2. The breath rhythm underlies the principle, contraction-release, used by Martha Graham.

3. The breath rhythm also underlies the principle of fall-recovery, used by Doris Humphrey. It is isolated by her in the term, speech phrase. She has remarked: "The breath rhythm in the time sense is a two-part phrase, the first longer than the second. In the space sense, it is a filling and expanding followed by a contraction. In the dynamic sense, it is a continuous movement growing in tension, followed by a letting-go of tension, which finishes with an accent." Doris Humphrey

4. "The trunk being the heaviest limb of the body, and that first influenced by emotion, owing to the action of the diaphragm, it follows that the most important and common instigator of all movements is the breathing. Breathing is at the basis of every manifestation of life, and plays as well aesthetically as physiologically, a role of the very highest importance in moving plastic. Movements may, however, have their starting-place in other parts of the body. The torso, arms, legs, hips, hands, shoulders, may alike give the impulse to the movement. And once the attitude is assumed with its starting-point in one or other of the limbs, breathing will assume the function of modifying the intensity of the arrested gesture." Note 6. See also under EURHYTHMICS.

See MOTOR PHRASE.

BROKEN CURVE. Used by the German-American dancer, Hanya Holm, to denote that movement wherein a curve relates itself to more than one center, as:

1. A curved movement is begun around a focal point and describes a half-circle, whereupon, instead of completing the circle, it moves off

and makes another half-circle around a second adjacent focal point. The line drawn by the moving member would approximate the letter S. There is no break at the point where the curved movement leaves the first circle and enters the second tangential circle. "Broken" here means a shift of focal point rather than a pause or break.

2. A curved movement is begun around a focal point and completes a half-circle, whereupon, instead of completing the circle, it retraces the same path backward to the starting point. In this case, a momentary pause naturally occurs before the direction is changed.

BROKEN FORM. One of the compositional forms used in the modern dance. Broken form denotes a series of movement-phrases that unfold and change with scarcely any repetition. A single movement-phrase may be repeated several times in succession but is then dropped and does not appear again in the dance. The movement-phrases would correspond to figures in music, a figure being described as "any short succession of notes, either as melody or a group of chords, which produces a single, complete and distinct impression." Note 7. Because of no form being inherent in such sequences, there must be something external to hold the dance together and this is found in drama: not drama in the sense of story, but rather of movement that can be identified with an object or an emotional situation. Broken form should never be used in an abstract dance. The latter would become monotonous and unintelligible if composed of a series of phrases that were never repeated elsewhere in the work. Doris Humphrey

Movement-phrases used in this manner constitute unitary ideas as distinguished from repetitive ideas. "It is difficult, however, to illustrate in Western music the distinction between unitary and repetitive ideas because most of its ideas are repetitive rather than unitary. Western music is in very essence repetitive, that is, the primary task of musical composition is to **use** every figure which is introduced by repeating it with suitable variations and transformations in other portions of the work." Note 8.

BROKEN STRAIGHT. When a movement in a straight line toward a given point is deflected from that point at an angle and seeks another point for conclusion, it may be called a broken straight. The line so drawn would result in any variety of right, acute, or obstuse angle. Hanya Holm.

CANON. In music, "the principle of a canon is that one voice begins a melody, which melody is imitated precisely, note for note, and generally, interval by interval, by some other voice, either at the same or a different pitch, beginning a few beats later and thus as it were running after the leader." Note 9.

In dance, the canon is used in a similar manner. In a two-voiced canon, the piano provides the first voice and the dancer the second, entering one measure later and reproducing the notes of the preceding measure in movement. The canon may also be the repetition by a group of dancers of a movement-phrase or group of phrases that have already been performed by a soloist who, simultaneously, has begun a new phrase. Other variations are possible and different coloring may be given to the movements depending upon whether it is the soloist or the group who is the leader.

CENTER OF MOVEMENT. A central point within the body from which all movement is considered to spring. This central point is conciously felt by the dancer, whether outwardly expressed or not, and gives vitality to the movement.

Isadora Duncan has remarked that "the ballet schools taught the pupils that this spring was found in the center of the back at the base of the spine. From this axis, says the ballet master, arms, legs and trunk must move freely, giving the result of an articulated puppet." Note 10. In academic ballet, the trunk was considered to be a more or less rigid pole whose two ends provided the basis for the movement of the arms and the legs. The trunk was infrequently used. Because of the emphasis on leg movement, the lower center was most frequently used.

It was Isadora Duncan who was to move this center to the upper chest. "For hours I would stand quite still," she has said, "my two hands folded between my breasts, covering the solar plexus. I was seeking and finally discovered the central spring of all movement, the crater of motor power, the unity from which all diversities of movement are born." Note 11. There was one obvious disadvantage to this shift from a lower to an upper center, i.e., arm movements increased enormously while leg movements decreased. The advantages, on the other hand, were incalculable. The focus of attention on the upper torso permitted a closer integration between arm and leg movements. It tended to make the torso a more flexible member than it had been previously. It called attention to the breath-rhythm as a rhythm that might underlie movement and give it coherence and led to the exploration of other natural rhythms such as rising and falling which is a concomitant of the breath-rhythm itself and, by extention, the wave rhythm, folding and unfolding, etc.

The modern dance made the center somewhat more flexible. It may be shifted according to the type and quality of the movement desired, from the chest to the solar plexus, the pelvis, the base of the spine, etc. The center may also be arbitrarily chosen: that is, movements of the arm, when the figure is in a crouched sitting position, may be made to appear in their action to be impelled from the pelvis as center. The use of any desired portion of the trunk as center allows both arms and legs to be used equally.

CENTRAL MOVEMENT. Any movement which refers from the outside to the nucleus; movement close to the body and in-drawn. No visible motion is necessary; any posture in which the main lines are consciously felt by the dancer as in-drawn may be central movement. Hanya Holm.

Antonym: PERIPHERAL MOVEMENT. See also CENTRIPETAL MOVEMENT, CLOSED MOVEMENT.

CENTRIFUGAL MOVEMENT. Movement impelled outward, as distinguished from centripetal movement which is movement drawn inward or directed toward a center. It is related to the path and curve in space where peripheral-pulling forces act on the body, the path being created through a revolving center, involving production of the spiral. Centrifugal movement is outward first at the summit and later at the base. Hanya Holm.

See also CENTRAL MOVEMENT.

CENTRIPETAL MOVEMENT. Movement drawn inward or directed toward a center, as distinguished from centrifugal movement which is movement impelled outward. It is related to the path and curve in space where center-pulling forces act on the body, the path being created through a revolving center, involving production of the spiral. Hanya Holm.

See also CENTRAL MOVEMENT.

CHANGE OF WEIGHT. Any shift of weight of the body from one member or point of the body to another, as in a walking step, a rocking step, etc.

CHOREGRAPHY. A system of signs and symbols devised to record dance or other movement on paper. The term should be discarded because of confusion with "choreography" and replaced by dance notation.

CHOREOGRAPHER. The person who constructs or designs a dance. The emphasis upon individualism and upon personal expression in the early phases of the modern dance, 1900-1940, led each dancer to feel obliged to be his own composer. It was only after this time that the distinction between performer and composer was recognized, as it had been for centuries in the field of music.

CHOREOGRAPHY. The art or science of composing a dance; the movements, phrases, rhythms, etc., and their construction and ordering constitute choreography. When first used in the early 18th century, choreography referred to a method of writing down a dance. This practice is now called dance notation; choreography is reserved to mean the art of composition in movement, whether the composition be written down or not.

CHOREUTICS. See SPACE, HARMONY IN.

CHOROSCRIPT. A new method of dance notation devised by Alwin Nikolais, who, having studied the Laban dance notation system in 1937 and finding it difficult in certain aspects, first presented his sytem in 1948. See Theatre Arts Monthly, February 1948, vol. xxxii, no. 2, pp. 63-66. "Nikolais adopted the musical note in its time implication, eliminating the necessity of the caliper-like reading that Laban's symbols require. The note symbol, with its stem serving as a directional indicator becomes a more flexible symbol, easier to manipulate on a staff-like graph without losing graphic quality. He employs a separation of the body graph into two staves, extremity and trunk . . . Nikolais has also devised a method of analysing and writing flexion, extension and rotation in one simple graphic series of 'accidental' symbols." Note 12.

Nikolais has remarked that "Choroscript represents the freezing of action at certain points so selected and so indicated that the symbols, read consecutively, give a clear and complete account of the movement. . . The stem of each note symbol indicates the spatial aspect (direction). . . Each symbol on the graph therefore indicates the time consumed in the movement, the nature of the movement (peripheral, rotary or locomotor) and the radial system to which, in which or through which the unit moves." Note 13.

See also LABAN DANCE NOTATION.

CIRCULAR MOVEMENT. A flow or current of curving movements without rhythmic cesuras; smooth, unbroken, legato. Since "circular" in itself implies a completed circle, and since circular movement is nearly always an arc or curve rather than a complete circle, the term "curved movement" seems more accurate and should replace the term "circular movement" unless the movement actually completes a circle.

CIRCULAR WAY. A term sometimes used to describe curved movements that pass through several directions in several planes in order to reach a pre-determined point. The term "indirect way" is preferred.

CIRCUMDUCTION. In general, a circuitous course; used in modern dance to describe the path of a body or any of its members in a curved movement through several planes, as: a movement of the right leg in a gesture close to the ground from in-place to diagonally-left-forward to diagonally-right-forward to straight-back to diagonally-right-back to side-right. Since this path is a variety of the "S" form, and since in physiology the term "circumduction" has the particular meaning of a complete circle, the term "indirect way" is to be preferred.

CIRCUMDUCTION, SIGNS FOR. Refers to eight signs in the Laban dance notation for the four diagonal directions deep and the four diagonal directions high which are used to plot the circuitous path on paper.

CLASSIC DANCE. Denotes the traditional ballet; occasionally applied to the Greek or Neo-Grecian dance. The term classic refers specifically to the codified technique of the ballet which was considered to be pure, correct, and refined. It denotes a style of dancing and has no association with the ancient Greeks or Romans. In the dance, it corresponds to the academy in the field of the fine arts.

CLOSED MOVEMENT. Term used by Hanya Holm to denote movement whose path is toward the body and whose force is diminishing. It involves the act of motion in a decreasing spatial area, whereas central movement, with which it is likely to be confused, involves the act of motion at the center. Closed movement goes toward the center; central movement occurs at the center. Centripetal movement, on the other hand, denotes movement impelled inward with the emphasis on rotation.

Antonym: OPEN MOVEMENT.

CODIFIED MOVEMENT. "Arbitrary sets of traditional, pre-conceived movements which form the basis for the technic of the ballet, as opposed to the free, highly personal, uncodified movements of the modern dance." Gertrude Lippincott. It will be essential for the modern dance to arrive at such a codification in order to continue itself.

COLLECT ONESELF. Used by Hanya Holm "to relate one's outer circumference to an imaginative center; to pull in to oneself, usually without visible movement; a magnetic attraction toward the center."
Similar in many respects to emotional tension, static tension.
This inner quality, experienced by all great dancers, was early stated by Isadora Duncan: "We do not know how to get down to the depths, to lose ourselves in an inner self, how to develop our visions into the harmonies that attend our dreams . . . We are ignorant of the repose of a descent, and the comfort of breathing, of mounting again, skimming, returning, like a bird, to rest." Note 14. In commenting upon some of her imitators, she said: "They copy the movements — but ignore the secret of the inner impulse." Note 15.

COMPOSITION SEMINAR. "A meeting of dancers and students at which finished dances or 'works-in-progress' are discussed and dissected from the point of view of their compositional aspects." Gertrude Lippincott.

CONCERT DANCE. 1) That type of dance which does not use the story form, plot and characters of the classic ballet, but which does use movement to convey emotions, or ideas as in absolute dance, etc.
2) Vaguely and indiscriminately applied to any dance, whether thematic or dramatic, which uses the modern dance technique, and to

any performance whether by a group or a soloist. This leads to confusion, since a soloist cannot give a concert, "concert" meaning little more than joint effort or performance. The term is undescriptive and should be abandoned.

See GROUP DANCE, SYMPHONIC BALLET, MUSIC-VISUALIZATION.

CONCERT GROUP. A number of professional dancers performing as support for a professional dancer or choreographer; also, such a group performing a group dance under the direction of a professional choreographer. The term is vague, but no other has been found to replace it except the term "dance company."

CONICAL HEIGHT. Denotes a movement beginning with an upward swing and concluding with a turn in which the body describes a cone, the head being the apex and the legs describing the circular base. Franziska Boas.

CONTINUOUS MOVEMENT. Self-evolving movement used by the modern dance; "the rhythm that rises, penetrates, holding in itself the impulse and the after-movement; call and response, bound endlessly in one cadence." Note 16. Movement throughout an entire dance or its various themes thus becomes an unbroken line rather than a series of dots and dashes. The term is somewhat ambiguous; is likely to be confused with "perpetual motion." Sequential movement is suggested to replace it.

CONTOUR. This refers to the characteristic or typical line that belongs to a particular style, as, in a broad sense, the shallow convex curve may be considered the characteristic line in Italian Renaissance painting. The word is used in conjunction with texture to determine style. The contour of Isadora Duncan's work might be described as a soft, indeterminate curve visible in the body at inhalation. The term is vague.

CONTRACTION. A drawing-together so that the size and the extent are diminished. Contraction is the physical process of shortening the distance between the two ends of a muscle. Such a contraction may occur within the arm, for example, without bending the arm. Contraction is the method and tension is the result.

See CONTRACTION-RELEASE.

CONTRACTION-RELEASE. Contraction-release, based upon the breath rhythm, is one of several expressions of the dynamic principles upon which the modern dance works; it has been mainly developed by Martha Graham.

"The two basic movements are what I call contraction and release. I use the term 'release' to express or denote the moment when the body is in breath, has inhaled, and has an aerial quality, and the term 'contraction' when the drive has gone down and out, when the breath is out." Martha Graham.

"The first principle taught, in floor exercises, is body center. The first movement is based upon the body in two acts of breathing — inhaling and exhaling — developing it from actual breathing experience to the muscular activity independent of the actual act of breathing. These two acts, when performed muscularly only, are called 'release,' which corresponds to the body in inhalation, and 'contraction,' which corresponds to exhalation. The word 'relaxation' is not used because it has come to mean a devitalized body." Note 17.

CONTRAPPOSTO. An Italian term denoting the twisting or spiral movement of the torso caused by the counter-direction of the members of the body. It is applied most specifically to the painting and sculpture of Michaelangelo in the High Renaissance in Italy. It has been suggested to indicate in modern dance any opposition of different members of the body which causes a twisting of the torso and thus differentiates between this type of movement and a simple opposition. The opposition of arm and leg in walking is called a simple opposition. In classical ballet, contrapposto has been made synonymous with opposition, but the ballet does not consciously use the opposition of the upper and lower body. To avoid confusion, a distinction between contrapposto and opposition should be made.

CONTRAPUNTAL MOVEMENT. See under COUNTERPOINT.

CONTRAST. The diversity of adjacent parts whether within the single body or within several bodies. The contrast, as of fast and slow, or soft and sharp, may occur simultaneously or in succession.

CONTROLLED MOVEMENT. Movement held at a conscious degree of tension and never permitted to dissipate itself.

See also SUSTAINED MOVEMENT.

CONTROLLED RELAXATION. A qualified term suggested to replace the term relaxation, since pure relaxation is rarely, if ever, used in a dance composition. Controlled relaxation denotes movement not obviously or visibly tensed; or the body at the smallest degree of tension possible while still under control and held in readiness for following movements.

COUNTERPOINT. 1. In music, "the name given to the art of combining melodies, or, (more strictly) to the art of adding melody to melody. The term is also often applied to the added melody itself, when a subject invented to accompany another subject is called its counterpoint." Note 18.

2. In modern dance, the combination of two movement-themes or phrases. Contrapuntal movement is that movement which has been added to the given movement.

CRESCENDO. An increase in force, as distinguished from accelerando which is an increase in time.

Antonym: DECRESCENDO.

CUMULATIVE FORM. One of the compositional forms used by the modern dance, as:

1. A movement-phrase increasing in tempo or intensity, as by doubling or tripling the beat;

2. Several phrases containing both fast and slow movements within themselves which have the lengths of the fast and the slow increased in each succeeding one;

3. A phrase begun by a single dancer and slowly imparted to the remainder of the group; or, in a single body, a phrase begun by one part of the body and repeated with the gradual addition of other parts. Doris Humphrey.

Also called ACCUMULATIVE RHYTHM.

CURVED MOVEMENT. A flow or current of curving movements without rhythmic cesuras; smooth, unbroken, legato movements using curved lines. This is suggested as a more accurate term than "circular movement," which implies a completed circle.

Antonym: ANGULAR MOVEMENT.

DALCROZE, EMILE JACQUES. See under EURHYTHMICS.

DANCE-CHOIR. See MOTION CHOIR.

DANCE CONCERT. A term used to denote performances mainly of group works or of the works of several choreographers. Neither this term nor dance recital has been completely satisfactory. In the presentation of works of a more theatrical character, such as Charles Weidman's Candide or Martha Graham's Deaths and Entrances, such terms as "dance theatre" or "modern ballet" have been used with little more success.

DANCE-DRAMA. Term suggested for the modern dance, as "a ballet" is used for the classical ballet; a dramatic dance involving a group of dancers and relating a story or dramatic idea.

See also BALLET, CONCERT DANCE, GROUP DANCE.

DANCE GRAMMAR. Dance technique or technical exercises.

DANCE NOTATION. The method of transcribing movements by signs and symbols written down on paper for preservation and dissemination. The signs and symbols so used are called dance script.

See also CHOROSCRIPT, LABAN DANCE NOTATION.

DANCE RECITAL. During the late 1920's and the 1930's, the term was applied to modern dance performances, possibly because so many of them, in the early stages of modern dance, were executed by soloists. The word "recital" generally means a performance by a single person, but may also mean the performance of the works of a single composer and thus could include group and solo works by one choreographer. In a program in which the work of several choreographers was presented, as in the Dance Repertory Theater, the term is no longer accurate. It was for this reason that the word "concert" was later used in place of the word "recital."

DANCE SCRIPT. The signs and symbols by which movements may be written down on paper. The art or practice of using these signs and symbols in order to transcribe movement is called orthography.

See also DANCE NOTATION, CHOROSCRIPT, LABAN DANCE NOTATION.

DANCE SYMPOSIUM. "A meeting of dancers and students at which a master lesson in technic, composition is given, along with a showing of students' dances, often with criticisms and suggestions. The form of the dance symposium varies greatly, but it is usually held by and for educational dance groups." Gertrude Lippincott.

DANCE WITHOUT MUSIC. "Just as music may or may not be accompanied by words, so the dance may, at least in theory, be either accompanied or unaccompanied by music. Here, however, we must be on our guard. Some auditory indication of the rhythm would seem to be quite essential; in the absence of music, dancers almost invariably rely on the rhythmic beat of a percussion instrument or its equivalent. The completely silent dance is even more of a tour de force than is wholly non-representational sculpture and painting, and is almost as unnatural as would be the use of words for literary effect without any regard to their meaning.

"Certain enthusiasts for the free dance feel that music, in contradistinction to a merely rhythmic beat, is not absolutely essential to the dance. Hanya Holm, for example, has not only solo dances which are entirely unaccompanied, but has one group number that depends exclusively on a common dance pulse. . . Unaccompanied dancing would certainly lose its expressive quality and become montonous if used for a full-length program. Wisely conceived and used, however, it can be extraordinarily effective. It is a safe generalization that music is made to contribute to the dance now as much as ever. Modern dancers are merely coming to a clearer realization of its proper function in the dance. It is extremely unlikely, however, that the musically unaccompanied dance will ever develop into a completely self-contained and expressive art form." Note 19.

Experiments in the creation of dances without musical accompaniment were first made by Mary Wigman in Germany in the 1920's and later in America by Doris Humphrey in the late 1920's and the 1930's. They were caused by the search for form through movement and reflect a general concern during this period for the purity of materials.

See also ABSOLUTE DANCE.

DECRESCENDO. A decrease in force, as distinguished from rallentando or ritardando which are a decrease in time.

Antonym: CRESCENDO.

DEEP. 1. Denotes in general any movement close to the floor.

2. Term used to describe movements of a certain type for dance notation and other purposes:

a. In the vertical body, any leg or torso movement below the horizontal plane which cuts through the hips and is parallel to the floor; or any arm movement below the horizontal plane which cuts through the shoulders and is parallel to the floor; or any foot movement, (step), with the knees slightly bent and the foot flat.

b. In other positions, all arm movement is considered in relation to the torso, as: with the legs vertical and the torso bent forward to right angles to the legs and parallel to the floor, if the arms are close to the torso and parallel with it, they are considered "deep" even though in a horizontal position. The torso here is "middle." All leg movement is considered in relation to the vertical body, as: in a sitting position with the torso and legs constituting a right angle, the legs are considered "middle" even though on the floor.

c. Note: We might consider the torso as a spool, the two ends being the horizontal planes through the shoulders and the hips. These two ends or planes always remain in the same relationship to the connecting tube in no matter what position the body may be tilted or bent. Thus the dimensions of the arm and leg movements may be immediately placed. The torso, however, is always considered in relation to an imaginary vertical line, or to the complete vertical body.

DELSARTE, FRANCOIS 1811-1871. The influence of Delsarte on gesture directly and on the modern dance indirectly has been generally acknowledged, but a great deal of research must be undertaken in order to establish the exact nature of that influence. It is at present most clearly affirmed in the German school. See Eukinetics, space harmony in. Delsarte analyzed gesture thoroughly and formulated a system of expression based upon it. "The Delsarte system tried to be the means of expressing mental phenomena by the play of the physical organs, the curling of the lip, the tossing of the head, the stamping of the foot, the turning in or out of the palm of the hand, the relaxing of an elbow, — each movement or attitude expressed something universally recognizable. Delsarte wrote voluminous notes, but never arranged or published them. The unedited writings were later published by Edgar S. Werner in New York . . . Steele Mackaye in

New York and Prof. Lewis B. Monroe in Boston spread the Delsarte system and its influence was felt in many fields. Among Mackaye's most enthusiastic converts was Genevieve Stebbins who went to Europe, talked with other pupils of Delsarte, and wandered through art galleries studying the attitudes of Greek statues and Renaissance paintings. Meanwhile, the Delsarte gestures and gymnastics found their way into most dancing schools. Isadora Duncan must have been influenced, perhaps unconsciously." Note 20. His system is based on a tripartite body, divided into an intellectual, an emotional, and a physical zone. Each of these zones may be further divided into three parts. All of them are conditioned by the three aspects of natural law: space, motion, and time. These various subdivisions resulted in nine laws of gesture. Upon these, Delsarte constructed a number of exercises so that each part of the body might be made fluid and expressive.

DESIGN. 1. Ordering; composing.

2. Design in time: a design in time is one which takes several counts or beats to be completed. "For a simple example, we might take the body that is moving in a straight line, while the arm is slowly rising and completing an arc over the head. It will take several footsteps before the arm has finished its pattern."

3. Design in space: a design in space refers to one which is presented instantaneously, without occupying several counts to be completed. It is "a movement seen only as an accent. Thus, a leap in the air is a design in space. It is the pattern of the figure in the air and not the few seconds of leaving the ground and returning to it which is remembered."

4. Design in dynamics: a design in dynamics refers to one, usually both in time and space, which emphasizes a crescendo or a decrescendo. "It is dynamism that controls the muscular phrase, that is, the succession of variations in movement which are performed on a sustained muscular impulse." Note 21. See also INTENSITY.

5. Combinations: designs in time and designs in space may be used separately, that is, with the greater emphasis on the one or the other aspect. However, all design is composed of both elements, and it is only the emphasis on one or the other which justifies the use of the separate term for a series of movements.

DETOUR. Applies to any movement which takes an indirect way through several planes to reach a given point.

See INDIRECT WAY, the preferred term.

DEVIOUS WAY. See INDIRECT WAY.

DIMENSIONS. The dimensions of a movement are especially useful in describing or notating that movement. In arriving at the dimensions of a movement, the following should be taken into consideration: direction, plane, time, and dynamics. For convenience, nine possible directions are used. The planes are divided into three categories: deep, middle, and high. The direction and the plane combined will place the movement accurately in space. Time is indicated by beat, count, or measure. Dynamics is indicated by qualifications of length or brevity, accelerando or diminuendo, staccato or legato, wide or narrow, strong or soft, etc. These four will accurately record the direction, space, time, and quality of the movement.

DIMINUENDO. A gradual diminishing in volume.

Synonym: DECRESCENDO; antonym: CRESCENDO.

DIRECTION. For describing a movement or writing it down in dance script, nine major directions are recognized: in place, forward, backward, side right, side left, diagonally left-forward, diagonally right-forward, diagonally left-back, and diagonally right-back. For further qualification, the planes are indicated according to deep, middle, or high. Illustrations: 1. The arms directly over the head are place-high; 2. The arms hanging at the sides are place-deep; 3. The arms at a diagonally forward position, shoulder high, are respectively diagonally-left-forward-middle and diagonally-right-forward-middle; etc.

See also DIMENSIONS.

DIRECTION INDICATORS. The name given to symbols in the Laban dance notation whose shape indicates the direction of the movement.

DISSOLVING. The flowing, smooth progression of one movement or sequence after another without perceptible break. The succeeding movement is initiated before the preceding movement dies. In the composition of group-units, it may be compared to a dissolve in the motion picture.

DISTORTED OPPOSITIONS. Used by the American dancer, Charles Weidman, and divided into three types.

1. "In the first case, he might use as a basis an oppositional movement through the body, where the leg is raised from the floor to the side, the opposite arm is extended horizontally for balance, and the head is turned to the side in opposition to the arm. This is a movement in space and takes place simultaneously in all the members. For distortion and accent, the movement is separated into its three parts: the leg is raised; then the arm; then the head: in quick succession so that it becomes a movement in time as well.

2. "In the second case, . . . he relies largely on the succession in time to hold the unrelated parts together and give them unity. Usually, if this is to maintain the continuity and not cause a break, it must be preceded by a well-established rhythmic continuity.

3. "The third case (deletion of the preparation) is very similar to the second, but may be applied to a single movement instead of to a phrase. For example, a leap in the air to the right is naturally preceded by a swing out to the left in preparation. . . . A distortion of this would simply be the execution of the leap itself with the oppositional preparation omitted." Note 22.

DISTORTED SUCCESSION. By "succession" is meant an unfolding of one part after another from a center, usually performed legato. By distorted succession is meant a staccato succession. Instead of the parts unfolding naturally and smoothly, they occur sporadically and are not naturally bound to any central point, but by careful selection, are made to appear to follow one another logically. For example, by eliminating several transitional movements in a succession, a distorted succession will result.

DISTORTION. Distortion refers to any deviation from the natural shape. "Nature has been decomposed . . . and remolded nearer to the heart's desire of the particular artist responsible for the process. If his heart happens to desire a state more sensuously pleasing than nature, we call his work beautiful and his process idealization; if he is of the obstreperous type which cares less for the sense reaction than for the communication of an emotional conviction, we may be inclined to call his work ugly and his process distortion. Whether it is beautiful or ugly depends upon the seeing eye, but the process is the same whichever its direction; it is a twisting out of the shape of nature." Note 23. Distortion is a form of abstraction; it is the result upon an object of accent and elimination.

DOWN-STROKE. Term suggested by Elizabeth Selden to make some correspondence between the downward movement in dance and the accented beat in music. She recognizes, however, that the accented beat does not necessarily require a downward movement but may be expressed by an upward one. The term is vague.

Antonym: UP-STROKE.

DRAMATIC DANCE. A composition in movement, with or without the accompaniment of music, arranged for action, and having a plot which culminates in a final situation or climax of human interest. The terms "dramatic dance," "pantomimic dance," and "abstract dance" tend to overlap in meaning. Generally, a pantomimic dance is one with characters and a well-defined plot of events, whose purpose is to tell a story. An abstract dance is one without characters or plot of events; its purpose is to convey a mood or an abstract idea. Dramatic dance is generally sandwiched between these two and partakes of the character of each. It plots not events but an idea or abstraction, and its characters are not persons but symbolic figures, generalizations, etc.

Charles Weidman's The Happy Hypocrite, 1931, relating the events of Max Beerbohm's story of that name and using named characters, scenes, dramatic unity, etc., may be called a pantomimic dance or a dance-pantomime. Doris Humphrey's Pleasures of Counterpoint, using movements one against the other to create a dynamic pattern or design, may be called an abstract dance. Esther Junger's Festive Rights, using a man and a woman in a generalized ritual of marriage and composed on a general dramatic thread of Processional, Betrothal, and Recessional, may be called a dramatic dance.

The three terms are occasionally helpful, never concise or definitive.

DUNCAN, ISADORA, THEORY. The most important terms associated with her are breath rhythm, center of movement, sequential movement, and wave rhythm. See also COLLECT ONE-SELF, CONTINUOUS MOVEMENT, DYNAMISM, GREEK DANCING, KINESTHESIA, RHYTHM. Those things listed under the theory of Charles Weidman are entirely associated with the stylization of pantomimic movement; those under the theory of Hanya Holm are directed toward the analysis of movement; those under the theory of Mary Wigman elaborate the subjective, emotional qualities of dynamic movement through physico-muscular means; those under the theory of Doris Humphrey are directed mainly toward composition for groups of dancers; those under the theory of Martha Graham enunciate a dynamic principle and indicate a content on the unconscious or subconscious level; those under the theory of Isadora Duncan state the emotional qualities of dynamic movement.

"Don't be merely graceful," Duncan has remarked. "Nobody is interested in a lot of graceful young girls. Unless your dancing springs from an inner emotion and expresses an idea, it will be meaningless and the audience will be bored." Note 24. "What must we do to bring Terpsichore back amongst us again? We must recover: 1: the ideal beauty of the human form; and 2: the movement which is the expression of this form. All my research and study in the field of the dance have been founded on these two principles. Always the lines of a form truly beautiful suggest movement, even in repose. And always the lines that are truly beautiful in movement suggest repose, even in the swiftest flight. It is this quality of repose in movement that gives to movements their eternal element. All movement on earth is governed by the law of gravitation, by attraction and repulsion, resistance and yielding; it is that which makes up the rhythm of the dance." Note 25.

DUNCAN DANCE. That form of natural dance using the plastic body governed by natural rhythms, adding gestures and attitudes borrowed from Greek vase paintings and fragments from Delsarte, and generally using music for interpretation. It is a weakened version of the principles laid down by Isadora Duncan and employs the simplest varieties of the walk, run, hop, skip, and leap.

Isadora Duncan founded schools in Berlin in 1904, in Paris in 1914, and in Moscow in 1921. Of all of the dancers taught by her, only the six girls known as the Duncan Dancers remained with her to maturity. Of these, Maria Theresa later formed a group called the Heliconodes, and Irma Duncan conducted the Russian school for a number of years, later returning to New York and publishing a textbook, The Technique of Isadora Duncan. Pupils of these pupils who have made a name for themselves have been Julia Levien, Anita Zahn, and Kathleen Hinni. "In May 1946 the Duncan Dance Guild published its first issue of the

Duncan Dance Bulletin, with the idea of further promoting and preserving the Duncan art intact." Note 26.

The Duncan dance is one form of romantic dance. Variations of the Duncan method are found in natural dance and Neo-Grecian dance.

DYNAMISM. 1. Any theory which views the universe as essentially or imminently constituted by forces.

2. Dynamism is one of the four distinctive elements of the modern dance, the other three being movement as substance, metakinesis, and form. John Martin was one of the first to state clearly the distinction between ballet and modern dance. Modern dance is actually dance presented in its fullest expression: a series of movements so ordered and composed as to express the subject matter; a series of movements, futhermore, that are evolutionary in the sense that they grow one from the other. This makes the dance a composition in sustained movement which may place no greater accent on the beginning and end of movement than on the interval that connects them. It dispenses with the static element that is inferred in poses and attitudes and substitutes for it dynamic flow. This led, early in the history of the modern dance, to the consciousness of pulsations in movement. The Germans, particularly Rudolf von Laban and Mary Wigman, stressed these pulsations in the term Anspannung und Abspannung — the ebb and flow of muscular impulse. This same quality lies behind Isadora Duncan's interest in the rhythms of the breath and the waves. These, and other American variations such as contraction-release and fall-recovery, contain within themselves periods of greater and of lesser tension. The dynamic element enters mainly in the giving of accent or stress which will usually mean an increase in the power or intensity of the movement.

3. Dynamics is the science of gradations of force, most apparent in modern dance through modifications of space. A section in Martha Graham's Primitive Mysteries might illustrate this, where she emerges from a surrounding group of dancers. If the group from which the dancer emerged were static, a certain dynamic effect would be produced. By having the group moving downward as she moves upward from the center, the dynamic effect is enormously increased.

4. "The basis of this philosophy is the dynamic comprehension of things: Being as a constant Becoming from the interaction of two

contrasting opposites. Synthesis, arising from the opposition between Thesis and Antithesis. The interaction of the two engenders and conditions Dynamism. The degree of distance determines the intensity of the tension. The form of this dynamics in space and time is Expression. The tension-stages are Rhythm. The dynamic comprehension of things is basic for the correct understanding of Art and all Art-forms. In the realm of art this dialectic principle of dynamics incarnates itself in Conflict as the fundamental basic principle of the substance of every Art-work and every Art-form." Note 27.

5. This interaction was first consciously used as a basic principle in dancing to natural rhythms, such as the rhythm of the blood, the breath rhythm, the wave rhythm, folding-unfolding, etc., and was later formulated by Rudolph von Laban in his theory of tension and relaxation. Although never clearly formulated by Isadora Duncan, the dynamic principle was nevertheless the basis of her work. In 1909 she stated: "And when we come to the movements of organic nature, it would seem that all free natural movements conform to the law of wave movement: the flight of birds, for instance, or the bounding of animals. It is the alternate attraction and resistance of the law of gravity that causes this wave movement." Note 28. That she early applied it to dance compositions may be glimpsed in an account by Margherita Duncan: "Early in her career, she conceived a dance typifying human experience which was like a mirror of her own subsequent life. It was not born of any piece of music, but of her own thoughts. She danced it sometimes, without music, and her audiences loved it and had named it Death and the Maiden after Schubert's song. In Paris the gallery never failed to shout for La Jeune Fille et la Mort at the end of a program, and once I saw her respond to that demand. We saw the gaiety of a youthful heart, suddenly stilled for a moment by a first apprehension of disaster — this fear thrown off and the gay business of life resumed — but the terror returning again and again until it overcame her, and she fell, defeated by forces stronger than herself. She called it The Maiden and Life." Note 29. In content and in the depiction of conflict, this early dance suggests many of the works created by Mary Wigman in Germany in the 1920's and 1930's. About 1909, Duncan remarked: "All movement on earth is governed by the law of gravitation, by attraction and repulsion, resistance and yielding; it is that which makes up the rhythm of the dance." Note 30.

EMOTIONAL TENSION. An emotional projection, not through visual means, or an inner vibration from which state abrupt gestures arise; these gestures are broken and not actually connected by transitional phrases. They seem right, logical and connected by the inner emotion or driving force that colors them. Typical examples may be found in the work of the Hindu dancer, Uday Shan-Kar or in staccato Hindu work in general. Such emotional tension is necessary in order to perform a distorted succession.

ENERGIZED ACTION. Term suggested by Elizabeth Selden to indicate movement impelled by energy and dynamic in character, as opposed to passive action in which the energy-drive is not apparent. Vague.

EUKINETICS. This is a third step toward the systematization of human movement. The systematization was begun by Delsarte in his analysis of pantomimic gesture, carried on by Rudolf von Laban in his studies of swings and the movements of the industrial worker. Eukinetics is a continuation of the tripartite character of the body which was divided by Delsarte into an intellectual, an emotional, and a physical zone and by Laban into high, low, or middle, depending upon the types of movement most suited to different bodies. It is directed toward control of dynamics and expression. Characteristic movements and gestures are evolved for the personality to be portrayed, whether it be classic, demi-caractère, or character. Movements are not only typical but may be conditioned so as to appear to increase or decrease the height of the dancer or suggest other qualities such as thinness or fatness, heavines or lightness, strength or weakness, etc. This system was evolved by Kurt Jooss.

Jooss divides all movement into either out-going or in-coming. This is very similar to Martha Graham's principle of contraction-release, although it is used for different purposes. These divisions he calls central and peripheral. They may be conditioned by intensity, strong or weak, and speed, slow or fast. Peripheral movements are further subdivided into drawing, floating, striking, and fluttering movements, conditioned by fast-slow and strong-weak. Central movements are subdivided into pressing, sliding, thrusting, and shaking movements, also conditioned by fast-slow and strong-weak. This permits movements to be begun in one category and changed in character by shifting from strong to weak to slow to fast.

The Laban system of swings has achieved artistic importance mainly through the absorption and transmutation of the system by Mary Wigman. The system of Eukinetics has produced so far no notable results unless one includes the Jooss Ballet's The Green Table, choreographed in 1932 for the Choreographic Competition held by the Archives Internationales de la Danse in Paris. No later work of the Jooss Ballet has equaled this one. This would seem to imply some weakness in the system itself. Its application has failed to produce any works of consequence since the initial effort.

EURHYTHMICS. Emile Jaques-Dalcroze, in his efforts "to broaden the basis of musical education and to make musical training a means of expression and not merely an end in itself; . . . gradually evolved his system of co-ordinating music and bodily movement. Working at it experimentally and unofficially with volunteer classes, he first gained public recognition of the method at a musical festival in Solothurn in 1905, and in the following year held the first training course for teachers. In 1910 he was invited to organize an institute for teaching rhythmical training in the garden suburb of Hellerau just outside Dresden, where he continued to develop his method on a gradually increasing scale until war broke out, when he returned to his native country and founded the Institut Jaques-Dalcroze at Geneva. He had already visited England with a group of pupils in 1912 . . . and in the following year the London School of Dalcroze Eurhythmics was founded under the directorship of Percy B. Ingham. Similar schools have been started in Paris, Berlin, Vienna, Stockholm, New York and other capitals.

"Its primary object is, in the words of its founder, 'to create by the help of rhythm a rapid and regular current of communication between brain and body, and to make feeling for rhythm a physical experience.' By developing, that is to say, the pupil's attention and powers of concentration and of eliminating all but the most essential muscular movements so that a kind of automatic technique is brought into play, the arms beat time, whilst the lower limbs indicate the note-values, the entire physical system is almost unconsciously controlled by the brain in response to the dictates of musical rhythm. After this training to obtain the pupil's rapid physical reaction to changing rhythms, given out by the teacher improvising at the pianoforte, comes a later stage when whole musical compositions are translated into a language of gesture and bodily movement. Bach's fugues,

Gluck's Orfeo and other works have in this way been given plastic expression by the Jaques-Dalcroze schools, and the principles underlying the method have been applied in varying degrees by others both to theatrical and to operatic productions." Note 31.

Jaques-Dalcroze mentions his indebtedness to Isadora Duncan, who herself repudiated his methods as too mechanical. His system has nevertheless had a profound effect upon the development of the dance. "We arrive at the conclusion," he says, "that the first place in the order of elementary music training should be accorded the muscular system. . . A child's body possesses instinctively the essential element of rhythm which is sense of time. Thus: 1. the beats of the heart, by their regularity, convey a clear idea of time, but they are a matter of unconscious activity, independent of the will, and therefore valueless for the purpose of execution and perception of rhythm. 2. The action of breathing provides a regular division of time, and is thus a model of measure. The respiratory muscles being subject to the will, in however qualified a degree, we are able to operate them rhythmically, that is to say, to divide the time and accentuate each division by a stronger muscular tension. 3. A regular gait furnishes us with a perfect model of measure and the division of time into equal portions. Now the locomotor muscles are conscious muscles, subject to absolute control by the will. We therefore find in walking the natural starting-point in the child's initiation into rhythm." Note 32.

See also MOTION CHOIR, MUSIC VISUALIZATION.

EXPRESSIONISTIC DANCE. A type of modern dance which is highly subjective and emotional and which expresses the dancer's feeling through movement. The externalization of the emotional experience through movement is achieved less by intellectual planning and more by "feeling through" with the body.

Expressionistic dance is akin to Expressionism in painting as revealed in the work of the Dutch painter, Van Gogh, or the German painter, Beckmann. During the twentieth century, it has been most completely a Teutonic expression in the dance. In this respect it is of interest to note that, in 1935, the German dancer, Harald Kreutzberg, considered this aspect of the dance to be the complete substance of the modern dance. He remarked that "the modern dance is a definite stylistic phenomenon, analogous to the appearance of expressionism in painting. It has as its aim the loosening of certain technical laws in favor of more salient emotional and atmospheric communication." Note 33. A statement by the German dancer, Mary Wigman, illuminates the powerful emotional character of this dance: "In performing my own dance compositions, the passionate desire arises in me at the moment of execution, to become one with these dances, to disappear in them, to live them." Note 34.

Although not calling the German dance expressionistic, Hanya Holm has made revealing comments about it. "The entire orientation of the dance of Mary Wigman is towards the establishment of a relationship between man and his universe... Emotionally the German dance is basically subjective and the American dance objective in their characteristic manifestations... The tendency of the American dancer is to observe, portray and comment on her surroundings with an insight lighted mainly by intellectual comprehension and analysis... The German dancer on the other hand starts with the actual emotional experience itself and its effect upon the individual. The distinction is one of 'being' as contrasted with 'doing' — of immersing the self in an emotional state as the necessary prelude to creation as contrasted with objective reconstruction of a known situation... In the German dance there is inherent the dangers of looseness of form, obscurity, and the attendant evils of mere self-expressionism. Properly controlled, however, and disciplined within its medium, this approach lends depth, radiance, and emotional conviction to the dancer's effort." Note 35.

For this reason, the German dance employs the principle of tension-relaxation which permits the widest possible spread between movement at its highest pitch and no movement. The expressionistic dance develops its movements very close to the two poles of tension and relaxation so that its contrasts are abrupt, when not violent. "This subjective and emotional approach colors even more subtly the use of space characteristic of the German dancer, it accounts at least in part for the greater consciousness of space, actual and created, as a factor of tremendous importance. Space, rhythm, volume, proportion are realized both by the American and the German dancer of first rank. But the use of space as an emotional element, an active partner in the dance, is distinctly European. Possibly because of a past more complex and a destiny more at the mercy of outer forces than is the case in America, we have become aware of the dramatic implications in the vision of the individual pitted against the universe. Space, with its constrictions and its immensity, its dark vistas and blinding horizons, becomes for the dancer an invitation or a menace, but in any case, an inescapable element." Note 36.

The American dancer, most of whose work can be called expressionistic, is Martha Graham. Her principle of contraction-release is closest to the German principle of tension-relaxation. It differs mainly in employing a narrower range and in depending more upon implication than statement.

EXTENSION. A stretching or lengthening to the fullest extent; a straightening of arm or leg so that the angle formed by the bones will be 180 degrees.

Antonym: FLEXION.

FALL-RECOVERY. One expression of the dynamic principle upon which the modern dance works; used particularly by Doris Humphrey. Fall-recovery is a synthesis resulting from the interaction of two opposites: a period of unbalance and a period of relative balance. Actually, there are three parts: a falling movement, a recovery, and a suspension, but the last two occur as one movement, the suspension being a hold at the peak of the recovery. All movement from the simple change of weight onward is an alternation between these two periods of balance and unbalance. The periods may be shortened or lenghtened. For example, in a quick falling run followed by a slow walk, the period of unbalance seems to occupy the complete length of the run, although obviously the run is composed of successive periods of balance and unbalance. By slightly exaggerating the falling tendency of the run and the erectness of the walk, the minor balances and unbalances are elided or glossed over. Their alternate succession and their respective lengths and stresses will provide the dynamic rhythm.

Doris Humphrey conceives movement, for the dancer's purpose, "to be basically one of equilibrium. In fact," she states, "my entire technique consists of the development of the process of falling away from and returning to equilibrium. This is far more than a mere business of 'keeping your balance,' which is a muscular and structural problem. Falling and recovering is the very stuff of movement, the constant flux which is going on in every living body, in all its tiniest parts, all the time. I recognized these emotional overtones very early and instinctively responded very strongly to the exciting danger of the fall, and the repose and peace of the recovery. Only much later did I find in Nietzsche a word expression of the meaning of these movements which revealed to me the fundamental rightness of my feeling. His two basic kinds of men, the Apollonian and the Dionysian, forever opposed and existing both in one man and in groups of men, are the symbols of man's struggle for progress on the one hand, and his desire for stability on the other hand. These are not only the basis of Greek tragedy, as Nietzsche pointed out, but of all dramatic movement, particularly dance. And dance movement should be fundamentally dramatic, that is to say, human, not decorative, geometric, or mechanical. The technique evolved out of this theory is amazingly rich in possibilities. Beginning with simple falls complete to the floor and recoveries to standing, many elements of movements reveal themselves in addition to the falling of the body in space. One of these is rhythm. In a series of falls and recoveries, accents occur which establish a rhythm, even a phrase, as the time-space is varied due to gravitational pull on the mass of the body. Another element is dynamism, that is, changes of intensity. A third element is design. Even the latter, usually considered to be linear, having nothing to do with movement, is a functional result of the body's compensatory changes. If left to itself, the body will make a number of weight adjustments in the course of a fall; and each of these will describe a design in space. These compensatory movements I call oppositions, and they occur in partial falls as well as in complete ones. For example, one foot will step forward to save the body on its way down; and at the same time, the arms will swing out. This is also true in walking, which is a partial fall. Each one of these elementary parts of movement is capable of more or less isolation and almost limitless variation." Note 37.

See also KINESTHETIC PHRASE, SPEECH PHRASE.

For other variations of the dynamic principle, see BREATH RHYTHM, CONTRACTION-RELEASE, FOLDING-UNFOLDING, TENSION-RELAXATION, WAVE RHYTHM.

FOLK FORM. One of the simplest compositional forms used by the modern dance, wherein two movement-themes are presented successively and are followed by a repetition of the first theme, with or without variations. Synonymous with ABA form, which is the better term of the two for clear understanding. See also SONG-FORM.

FLEXION. Generally denotes a bending with tension at the elbow or knee joint decreasing the angle formed by the bones; may also refer to a raising of the arm or leg by a movement at the shoulder or hip joint, or to a bending of the body whereby the back is rounded and the shoulders and hips are brought closer together.

Antonym: EXTENSION.

FLOOR-PATTERN. The design traced on the floor by the dancer's feet; also called floor-track.

FLOOR-TRACK. See FLOOR-PATTERN.

FOLDING-UNFOLDING. Folding-unfolding, used in different ways by different systems, was little more than a variation of tension-relaxation based on forms in nature. Folding is a sinking, drooping, or relaxing of the body as muscular energy is withdrawn from the various parts of the body. It may result in an inward stillness or a bodily relaxation while the body remains upright, or it may be carried to an extreme where the body slowly sinks from an upright position to a horizontal position on the floor in a relaxed fall. Unfolding is the opposite of this, where the body, in response to renewed muscular energy, opens up or unfolds in the manner of a flower. This may occur in a sitting position, or it may involve the lifting of the body from a horizontal to a vertical position.

Folding-unfolding is one variety of the fundamental dynamic principle of the counteraction of two opposites. It is a variant of tension-relaxation, contraction-release, and fall-recovery, but is considerably weaker through being too imitative of things in nature.

FREE DANCE. Denotes modern dance as distinguished from classic ballet; term originated by Elizabeth Selden to apply to all types of dancing that broke from the tradition of the classic ballet in the manner of Isadora Duncan.

Except as it indicates freedom from the previous technical code, "free" has no particular meaning. The term is not commonly used and should be discarded as vague.

See MODERN DANCE.

FREE LEG. That leg which is not bearing the body-weight.

Antonym: SUPPORTING LEG.

FUGUE. 1. In music, "a musical movement in which a definite number of parts or voices combine in stating and developing a single theme, the interest being cumulative. . . The main idea of a fugue is that of one voice contrasting with others." Note 38.

2. In dance, a similar development using movements and movement-phrases.

FUNCTIONAL MOVEMENT. Refers to all movement of the modern dance which has its own peculiar place and function within the scheme of the dance; movement used as a means of expression; movements related to other movements and so connected that no change can be made without producing a corresponding change in other movements. More generally, a movement both kinetic and metakinetic, that is, with overtones of meaning and expression.

Functional movement refers to movement as the substance of the dance, or to what Mary Wigman calls "pure movement. Charged as I frequently am," she remarked in 1931, "with freeing the dance from music, the question often arises, what can be the source and basic structure of my own dancing. I cannot define its principles more clearly than to say that the fundamental idea of any creation arises in me or, rather, out of me as a completely independent dance theme. This theme, however primitive or obscure at first, already contains its own development and alone dictates its singular and logical sequence. What I feel as the germinal source of any dance may be compared perhaps to the melodic or rhythmic subject as it is first conceived by a composer, or to the compelling image that haunts a poet. But beyond that I can draw no parallels. In working out a dance I do not follow the models of any other art, nor have I evolved a general routine for my own. Each dance is unique and free, a separate organism whose form is self determined. Neither is my dancing abstract, in intention at any rate, for its origin is not in the mind. If there is an abstract effect it is incidental. On the other hand my purpose is not to interpret the emotions. Grief, joy, fear, are terms too fixed and static to describe the sources of my work. My dances flow rather from certain states of being, different stages of vitality which release in me a varying play of the emotions, and in themselves dictate the distinguishing atmospheres of the dances." Note 39.

GERMAN DANCE. The modern dance in Germany, until its life was abruptly ended by the Nazi regime, is mainly the stories of Rudolf von Laban and Mary Wigman. Isadora Duncan had danced; Delsarte and Dalcroze had stated and disseminated their theories. "The decisive problem was to bring the creative impulse, the artistic urge for expression into immediate organic connection with movement. The actual question for the dancer was how to turn her dance vision into a congruent form of motion that would express that vision, and that vision only, with complete integration and perfection. . . . It was this question that Mary Wigman was the first to ask herself with unrelenting insistence." Note 40. At approximately the same time, the same question was being answered in America by Doris Humphrey and Martha Graham.

"The way from conception to realization was long and hard. Mary Wigman achieved it with the help of Rudolph Von Laban's theory. Laban's discovery may be expressed in a few words. He recognized the legitimate connections between the structure of the human body and its capacity for direction and motion. Though different in results, the laws of movement are the same as those that govern everyday life in work, sport, dance, or gymnastics. All the possibilities of direction and destination that are available to man in general, are available to the dance. Instead of the predetermined gestures and poses of the ballet, Laban set up the natural, dynamic urge-to-motion that impels the dancer to the space-rhythmic self-discharge as the Alpha and Omega of dancing. From this conception of the function of the urge-to-motion, it follows that the dance movement is genuinely significant only in so far as it is an expression of the entire personality, the active inner life of the dancer. Thus this theory of the dance demands as its first principle, the self-expression of the dancer's personality." Note 41. "As an artist, Mary Wigman was enabled, through her German nature, to attain in dancing the pre-eminence held by all real German art, that of expression as opposed to form. This is accomplished, not by disdaining or destroying form, but by infusing it with life so that it dissolves into the intensity of expression." Note 42.

The subjective and emotional character of the German dance has been frequently stressed by Mary Wigman. She has stated that "all dance construction arises from the dance experience which the performer is destined to incarnate and which gives his creation its true stamp. The experience shapes the kernel, the basic accord of his dance existence around which all else crystallizes. Each creative person carries with him his own characteristic theme. It is waiting to be aroused through experience and completes itself during one whole creative cycle in manifold radiations, variations and transformations." Note 43.

The modern dance in Germany, as in America, was to be based upon a core of natural movements. Movement itself was to be the substance of the dance. In order to make this fact incontrovertible, Mary Wigman was the first to compose and perform a dance entirely without music. The dynamic principle, in these and in the dances with accompaniment as well, was that of tension-relaxation. Partly because of the German predilection for themes that concerned man in conflict within or with his universe, themes occasioned by the exhaustion of Germany after World War I, and partly because of the continuous character of the movements analyzed by Laban, such as the figure 8 traversed by the series of swings elaborated by him within the framework of an icosahedron, space was always an active agent in the German dance. "Mary Wigman, from whose genius and early experiments the entire German dance derived its present standing illustrates perfectly this intimate feeling for space. . . In her dance she alternately grapples with space as an opponent and caresses it as though it were a living, sentient thing. In her gestures and movements she carves boldly and delicately visible and fluid forms, shaping, surrounding, and sinking in the space which presses close above her." Note 44.

Space became the omnipresent partner in the dance; it was an immeasurable fluid made palpable. The living partner contended with it and succumbed to it — tension and relaxation, conflict and death. The German dance, as represented in the work of Wigman, was thus a flowering in movement of the space obsession which has characterized western culture and had already received full expression in the other arts. In the dance, the soul of man, the ego, the sense of the infinite and the sense of becoming were finally made manifest.

This raises questions which it is beyond the scope of this lexicon to answer in any detail. Why was it not the ballet which was to arrive at a complete western expression? Why, if it expresses the culmination of a culture, was the German vocabulary of movement hailed as new and revolutionary? Ballet technique, in its defiance of gravity, was continually concerned with space. The restriction of movement to the extremities, however, prevented the ballet, up to the end of the 19th century, from attaining mature expression for which it needed a more natural movement with its focal point in the torso. It is more than probable that the ballet will achieve such an expression in the 20th century. Isadora Duncan was the first to reveal to it new possibilities. Nijinsky, if he had not gone insane, might well have effected the revolution. If it is to be done, it will be in England or America through a development of the work of such choreographers as Antony Tudor. For the second question, the revolutionary character of the modern dance vocabulary, the answer may not be too difficult. The insistence upon natural movement by Isadora Duncan, by Mary Wigman, by all modern dancers does not mean that a stipulated series of natural movements is the vocabulary of all modern dancers, but rather that natural movements and rhythms are the basis of whatever stylized, personalized, or distorted movements each dancer may evolve. It thus becomes perfectly possible for the basis of a technique to be revolutionary at the same time that its expression may be a continuation of an established tradition and belief. In this sense, the German dance, while using movement different from that codified by the ballet through the centuries, directed its movement toward an expression of an exhausted culture. It is of more than passing interest that Laban should be greatly concerned with the spatial implications of movement and that tension-relaxation should be the dynamic principle of the German dance.

The dynamic principles so far enunciated in America have closer poles than the German and do not permit the element of no-movement implied in relaxation to enter. The absence of space in the German sense has been commented upon and regretted. The absence, however, would seem to be due not to neglect but rather to the very nature of the dynamic principles that the American dancer found it necessary to employ. The differences between the German and the American dance were already felt in 1935 by Hanya Holm who remarked that "the tendency of the American dancer is to observe, portray and comment on her surroundings with an insight lighted mainly by intellectual comprehension and analysis... The German dancer on the other hand starts with the actual emotional experience itself and its effect upon the individual. The distinction is one of 'being' as contrasted with 'doing'." Note 45. It is this shift of emphasis which may mark the distinction between a dance that looks backward and a dance that looks forward, or between a dance that culminates a culture and a dance that presages a new culture. Time must elapse before these distinctions can be affirmed and made clear.

The German approach has been generally unsuccessful when called upon to handle groups as elements of creative choreography. Individualism was too strong. Arthur Michel, on commenting in 1935 on the use of the group by Wigman in 1923, makes a revealing statement: "There seemed to be perfect agreement between will and technical power; in this case between the will of the leader and the power of the pupils." Note 46. Group movement was to find itself only in mass dancing, a kind of artistic calisthenics that was to serve as an answer to the physical and spiritual crises of World War I. "The essence of the German art ideal today, 1931, lies in the stimulation to activity of the public itself, in the development of a receptivity to experience which shall create a new social culture. Such a conception always seeks contacts with primitive culture and, by bodily appropriating primitive forms, it attempts to reconstruct the ideal conditions of savage ceremonial art. Its adherents busy themselves with the vestiges of religious dances in Africa, grow intoxicated at the mystic power discernible in the dances of Java and India, and respectfully scrutinize the backgrounds of the Japanese and Chinese theatres. They also investigate their own land and find traces of ancient cults in its national ceremonies and in its folk customs and dances. The contrast between actor and spectator disappears, the frame of the stage is shattered. Whoever participates in this common experience cooperates in the ritual. Here we must record the most important event in the dance revolution: the creation of the 'Bewegungschor' the chorus of lay dancers, a new type of non-professional activity, established by Rudolf von Laban." Note 47.

For further elaboration of aspects of the German dance, see under Laban, Wigman, absolute dance, dance without music, expressionistic dance, motion choir space, (space harmony in), tension-relaxation.

Many of the terms defined by Hanya Holm will be further reflections of the German dance, tempered by America. Some of these are axial movement, balance, broken curve, broken straight, centrifugal movement, centripetal movement, closed movement, collect oneself, open movement, peripheral movement, relaxation, step-scale, straight movement, tension.

GESTURE. A movement by any member of the body without a transfer of weight. The term is also used in a broader sense by Doris Humphrey to denote the patterns of movements that have been evolved by human beings and that have come down as an inherited language. These, through stylization, are available to the dancer.

In its broadest definition, gesture denotes any expressive movement of the body. In a narrower sense, it denotes expressive movements of the arms or head. In the 19th century, gesture was closely studied and analyzed by Delsarte. His analyses have caused Rudolf von Laban to divide dancers into high dancers, low dancers, and middle dancers and to arrange movement-scales for each type. The influence of Delsarte is also acknowledged in Kurt Jooss' development of Eukinetics.

See SPACE, HARMONY IN.

GRAHAM, MARTHA, THEORY. One of the three dancers emerging from the Denishawn School who established the modern dance in America. Graham left the Denishawn School in 1923 and evolved her own style by 1929. The most important terms associated with her are contraction-release, motor memory, and percussive movement. See also posture, release. Those things listed under the theory of Charles Weidman are entirely concerned with the stylization of pantomimic movement; those under the theory of Hanya Holm are directed toward the analysis of movement: those under the theory of Isadora Duncan state the emotional qualities of dynamic movement; those under the theory of Mary Wigman elaborate the subjective, emotional qualities of dynamic movement through physico-muscular means; those under the theory of Doris Humphrey are directed mainly toward composition for groups of dancers; those under the theory of Martha Graham enunciate a dynamic principle and indicate a content on the unconscious or subconscious level.

GREEK DANCING. 1. Commonly, the dance developed and used by the Greeks from the seventh through the fourth centuries B.C.

2. The term is also applied to dances which attempt to imitate or

reconstruct the Greek dance in later periods. Since all movement in Greek dancing during the twentieth century has been perforce arbitrarily reconstructed, the use of the term "Greek dancing" for this reconstruction is confusing and incorrect. The term "Neo-Grecian dance" would more strictly define those schools which followed Greek modes. The revival of Greek dancing was due to Isadora Duncan's turning back to mature classical Greek art as a source of inspiration during the first quarter of the twentieth century. It was never her purpose, however, to reconstruct Greek dances. She has said: "The dance, to be art for us, must be born out of ourselves, out of the emotions of the life of our times, just as the old dances were born out of the life and emotion of the ancient Greeks." Note 48. Nevertheless, a number of Greek schools sprang into being and led to such things as, in 1923, the establishment of the Greek Dance Association of Stratford-on-Avon in England to codify the teaching of the Greek dance.

3. Modern dancers have used the Greek dance only in the sense indicated by Isadora Duncan. This is part of the movement back to primitive forms so apparent in the field of contemporary painting.

GROUP. A number of dancers performing a single composition. Such a group working under a professional dancer and performing with him is called a concert group. A group of lay dancers is called, in Germany, a motion choir. In general, the group is to the modern dance as the corps de ballet is to the ballet.

HEALTH DANCING. Dancing whose sole purpose is to give exercise to the body; a kind of rhythmic gymnastics to increase the health and vigor of the body.

Synonym: NATURAL DANCE.

HEAVY-POINT. The center of gravity in the body which is considered to be in the pelvis. Rudolf von Laban

HIGH. 1. Denotes generally any movement which has an upward tendency, above the head.

2. Denotes particularly, in reference to Laban dance notation:

a. In the vertical body: Any leg movement above the horizontal plane that cuts through the hips and is parallel to the floor; the vertical, erect torso; any arm movement above the horizontal plane that cuts hrough the shoulders and is parallel to the floor.

b. In other positions: All arm movement is considered in relation to the torso, as: with the legs vertical and the torso bent forward at right angles to the legs and parallel to the floor, if the arms are forward and in direct line with the torso, they are considered "place-high," even though they are in a horizontal plane which, for the vertical body position, would make them "middle." All leg movements are considered in relation to the vertical body.

c. Note: The torso might be considered as a spool whose two ends constitute the two horizontal planes through the shoulders and the hips. These two ends or planes always remain in their same relationship to the connecting tube no matter in what position the body may be tilted or bent. Thus, the dimensions of the arm and leg movements may be immediately placed. The torso, however, is always considered in relation to an imaginary vertical line, or to the complete vertical body.

HIGH DANCER. One of the three types of dancer, as named by Rudolf von Laban, the other two being middle dancer and low dancer. The distinction is based on general physique which determines the variety of movement most used. A high dancer will be generally tall and thin and will find light aerial movement with great extensions most natural to his physique.

HOLM, HANYA, THEORY. An artist trained in Germany under Mary Wigman and achieving her own style in America in the 1930's after adapting the German technique to American conditions. Terms associated with her are axial movement, balance, broken curve, broken straight, central movement, centrifugal movement, centripetal movement, closed movement, collect oneself, open movement, peripheral movement, relaxation, step-scale, straight movement, tension, tension-relaxation. Those things listed under the theory of Charles Weidman are entirely concerned with the stylization of pantomimic movement; those under the theory of Doris Humphrey are direced mainly toward composition for groups of dancers; those under the theory of Martha Graham enunciate a dynamic principle and indicate a content on the unsconscious or subsconscious level; those under the theory of Isadora Duncan state the emotional qualities of dynamic movement; those under the theory of Mary Wigman elaborate the subjective, emotional qualities of dynamic movement through physico-muscular means; those under the theory of Hanya Holm are directed toward the analysis of movement.

HORIZONTALITY. Term referring to the stress on horizontal line in any movement or movement-phrase.

HUMPHREY, DORIS, THEORY. One of the three dancers emerging from the Denishawn School who established the modern dance in America. Humphrey left the Denishawn School in 1928, when, in conjunction with Charles Weidman, she gave her first New York recital. Her style had already begun to take form during her teaching days at Denishawn. The most important term associated with her is fall-recovery. See also balance-unbalance, breath rhythm, broken form, cumulative form, design, kinesthetic phrase, movement, music-visualization, opposition, recurring theme, repetitious form, rhythm, selective form, speech phrase, succession, unison. Those things listed under the theory of Martha Graham enunciate a dynamic principle and indicate a content on the unconscious or subconscious level; those under the theory of Charles Weidman are entirely concerned with the stylization of pantomimic movement; those under the theory of Hanya Holm are directed toward the analysis of movement; those under the theory of Isadora Duncan state the emotional qualities of dynamic movement; those under the theory of Mary Wigman elaborate the subjective, emotional qualities of dynamic movement through physicomuscular means; those under the theory of Doris Humphrey are directed mainly toward composition for groups of dancers.

ICOSAHEDRON. A geometric device used by Rudolf von Laban to exemplify his theory of the harmony of space. "The Laban Method uses a 'life-size' icosahedron apparatus literally, in which movements are performed. Geometrically speaking, the icosahedron is a perfect symmetrical polyhedron: the most perfect geometrical form approaching the sphere and related to the cube." Note 49. It consists of twenty equilateral triangles meeting at twelve points.

For the development of swings within this geometrical form, see SPACE, HARMONY IN.

IMPULSE MOTIONS. Weighted movements propelled dynamically from the center of the body. A better term is percussive movement.

INDIRECT WAY. The path of a body or any of its members in a curved movement through several planes; a circuitous course followed by some member of the body, as: a movement of the right leg in a gesture close to the ground from in-place to diagonally-left-forward to diagonally-right-forward to straight-back to diagonally-right-back to side-right.

Synonym: DETOUR, DEVIOUS WAY. The term "indirect way" is to be preferred.

INTENSITY. Degree of stress in movement. Variations in intensity from weak to strong provide the pulsations or the ebb and flow of muscular impulse from which grow the phrases and rhythms of the dance. The degrees of stress are the dynamics of modern dance movement. Charles Weidman states that "intensification denotes the meaning; that a movement by itself, that is, in a generalized form, contains no meaning whatever." Note 50.

INTERPRETIVE DANCE. In the 1920's and 1930's, interpretive dancing was defined as a form of modern dance that combined music-visualization and expression. Interpretive dancing should not, although it often did, use pantomimic movement to illustrate parts of the music. It was defined by Elizabeth Selden as a work composed by a dancer with an intimate knowledge of musical structure, a strong rhythmic sense, and an ability to work in movement patterns. Such a composition would be the translation of an aural strucure into a visual one. In this sense, interpretive dancing would be synonymous with music-visualization. Unfortunately the definition of the word "interpret" as "to explain the meaning of" often sidetracked this pure aim. Interpretive dancing was usually an excuse for emoting to music with results that were banal when not embarrassing. Interpretive dancing has now taken on a more restricted meaning as the more or less verbatim translation of music into movement based on the musical rhythm. The method has been severely criticised since music is self-contained and does not need re-expression in another medium. In modern dance, it reached its height during the 1920's and 1930's when the incipient modern dance, searching for formal structure, leaned heavily upon music for support. The method was taken over by the classic ballet in the 1930's and 1940's under the name "symphonic ballet."

See MUSIC-VISUALIZATION.

ISOLATION. Intense concentration upon isolated parts of the body. Movement of the whole body is kept constantly in mind, but stress is also laid upon each of the parts. This may be achieved through an exercise specifically directed toward that part, or through an exercise of larger dimensions where now one and now another part become the focal point. The purpose is to increase awareness of the possibilities and potenialities of each part of the body and to sharpen and strengthen the movement. José Limon.

JAQUES-DALCROZE, EMILE. See under EURHYTHMICS.

JOOSS, KURT. See under EUKINETICS.

KINESIS. Physical movement, whose psychical accompaniment is meta-kinesis.

KINESTHESIA. "The sense whose end organs lie in the muscles, tendons, and joints and are stimulated by bodily tensions; the muscle sense." Note 51.

". . . a sixth sense, whether it exists officially or not among those who live by the book, functions most serviceably. It is primarily a muscle sense and is called kinesthesia—'movement-perception.' Embedded in the tissue of the muscles and in the joints there are sense organs which respond to movement much as the organs of seeing respond to light. . . However, in conjunction with the semicircular canals in the ears, which tell us a good many useful things about balance, posture, and position, these humble organs, that have never been given anything but the generic name of proprioceptors, make it possible for us to know our own movement at first hand without seeing, hearing, touching, tasting, or smelling it. We can ascertain quite without effort whether we are upside down or rightside up, and be perfectly aware of the relation of one part of the body to another. Through the agency or kinesthesia we are also made, though not always consciously, to associate experiences of all sorts with the bodily movements which accompany them, and to apply the fruits of this union to such an incalculable number of everyday contacts as to set up whole systems of practice. . . When we see a human body moving, we see movement which is potentially producible by any human body and therefore by our own; through kinesthetic sympathy we actually reproduce it vicariously in our present muscular experience and awaken such asso-

ciational connotations as might have been ours if the original movement had been of our own making. . . . This is not a new demand which
has been made exclusively by the modern dance, though the modern
dance, in that it deals with more vital stuff than the academic dance,
has naturally made heavier calls upon it and brought it correspondingly
more into the foreground of attention." Note 52.

The modern dance has not only made heavier calls upon it; it has
based its movement upon natural rhythms and has stressed the
sequenial flow of that movement. Its movement is therefore more
naturally referable to the movement-potentialities of the average
human being. Kinesthesia was recognized, although not named, in an
essay published in 1928 by Margherita Duncan who wrote: "The first
time I ever saw Isadora Duncan she was dancing on the Carnegie Hall
stage to the music of Gluck's Iphigenia. I experienced what I can only
describe as an identification of myself with her. It seemed as if I were
dancing up there myself. This was not an intellectual process, a critical
perception that she was supremely right in every movement she made;
just a sense that in watching her I found release for my own impulses
of expression; the emotions aroused in me by the music saw themselves translated into visibility. Her response to the music was so true
and inevitable, so free from personal eccenricity or caprice, her self-
abandonment to the emotion implicit in the music so complete that
although I had never seen nor imagined such dancing, I looked at it
with a sort of delighted recognition. I think this experience of mine
must have been common among her audiences; for the desire for
beauty lies at the bottom of every human heart and she gave it expression, so that in watching her we had a sense of satisfied longing."
Note 53.

Kinesthesia has a subconscious as well as a conscious level; each
human being possesses a motor memory, usually submerged but
capable of being brought to the conscious level. It is implied in
Margherita Duncan's statement above that, "although I had never seen
nor imagined such dancing, I looked at it with a sort of delighted
recognition." It conditioned many of the compositions of Martha Graham, particularly during the 1940's. "She wanted to go back through
motor memory to the ancestral moods to find an explanation of what
we are today." See motor memory. It was implied in a statement
by Isadora Duncan in 1903 that, "if we seek the real source of the

dance, if we go to nature, we find that the dance of the future is the dance of the past, the dance of eternity, and has been and always will be the same." Note 54. It was recognized by a statement of Shaemas O'Sheel in 1928: "Symbolic art goes back through Time even to beginnings that are forgotten; evades the ephemeral and twines like a tendril about the lessential, drawing sustenance from all great moments; penetrates below surfaces, through flesh and nerves to the quick core of being; taps the very sources of joy and grief, and startles from their slumber those race-memories that live unnoted in the still places of the soul. Let the wise of future generations understand that more than any other of this age, Isadora was the naive companion and messenger of the stars and the sword, the rose and the rood, mystery, and wonder, and eternity." Note 55.

In 1920, Isadora Duncan remarks, in reference to music composers: "There are those who, subconsciously, hear with their souls some melody of another world, and are able to express this in terms comprehensible and joyous to human ears." She continues: "Imagine then a dancer who, after long study, prayer and inspiration, has attained such a degree of understanding that his body is simply the luminous manifestation of his soul; whose body dances in accordance with a music heard inwardly, in an expression of something out of another, a profounder world. This is the truly creative dancer, natural but not imitative, speaking in movement out of himself and out of something greater than all selves." Note 56.

KINESTHETIC PHRASE. "The way of moving the body by its physical possibilities. Change of weight is the beginning of movement. The kinesthetic phrase becomes monotonous and repetitious with shifting body weights. Its final result, if it were used entirely by itself, would be nothing more than physical exhaustion. It is the speech phrase that provides rhythm." Doris Humphrey.

See also FALL-RECOVERY.

KINESTHETIC RESPONSE. The response of one person to the movement of another. "The dance exists exclusively in terms of the movement of the body, not only in the obvious sense that the dancer moves, but also in the less apparent sense that its response in the spectator is likewise a matter of body movement. . . . When we see a human body moving, we see movement which is potentially producible by any human body and therefore by our own; through kinesthetic sympathy we actually reproduce it vicariously in our present muscular experience and awaken such associational connotations as might have been ours if the original movement had been of our own making." Note 57.

KINETIC. Of, pertaining to, or due to motion.

KINETIC PANTOMIME. Term used by Charles Weidman to indicate pantomimic movement subjected to the laws of abstract movement: ordered, composed, accented, repeated, contrasted, and distorted. "I use the term Kinetic Pantomime as opposed to dramatic pantomime, whereby the play of bodily members and of facial mobility convey ideas or tell a story. Kinetic Pantomime deals with movement of the whole body. It rhythmizes this movement and gives it the basis I use for dance composition. It is pure dance movement stylized into pantomimic form; it does not become absolute pantomime. In its ideal state it might be considered a fusion of abstract and pantomimic qualities." Charles Weidman

KINETOGRAPHIE LABAN. The method of dance devised by Rudolf von Laban; see under LABAN DANCE NOTATION.

LABAN, RUDOLF VON. A Hungarian-born teacher whose analysis of movement was codified in a series of swings developed within a geometrical form, the icosahedron. The swings, worked out in various movement-scales, are of importance because of their space-evoking qualities. Inasmuch as they are based upon the continuous line of a figure 8, it is probable that the weaving character of this line through a number of spatial directions tends to create a tangible space. See space, harmony in. Laban's analysis had been developed by the time Mary Wigman studied with him in 1913. His methods had profound effect upon her and contributed to her own development of spatial quality in movement. Others influenced by him have been Kurt Jooss and Sigurd Leeder who systematized the Laban principles further in Eukinetics.

In his subdivision of dancers, Laban was influenced by Delsarte. He classified them according to high, middle, or low, according to the type of movement that was most natural to them. It was this classification which prompted Jooss to experiment in the direction of dynamics and expression and evolve Eukinetics.

In 1928, Laban published a system of dance notation called Schrift- tanz which, two years later, was translated into English and French. Of all methods developed since the fifteenth century, this seems the most complete for recording all types of dances. See LABAN DANCE NOTATION. In 1945, Laban adapted his notation for industrial purposes to check gains and losses through different kinds of movement. Laban's notation was first seriously presented in America by Irma Otte-Betz and Irma Dombois-Bartenieff who published a series of simple exer- cises under the title of Elementary Studies in Laban's Dance Script in 1937 and taught the method. In 1940 a number of students of the method, Henrietta Greenwood, Ann Hutchinson, Janey Price, and Helen Priest, incorporated their knowledge and efforts and formed the Dance Notation Bureau in New York. Within this group, Hildegard Blum has brought out A Primer for Dance Notation which forms a good introduction to the revised system.

LABAN DANCE NOTATION. In 1928, Rudolf von Laban published his method of dance notation under the title of Schrifttanz. Although it has undergone considerable modification since that time, it remains the most important and all-inclusive system that has appeared.

Movements are recorded on a musical staff set vertically on the page and read from bottom to top. The main symbols are based on a rectangle and its variations. The rectangular symbol drawn between two lines of the staff indicates "in position." The length of the rectangle gives its time-value. Approximately a quarter of the area removed at one end will give a simplified pointing hand: removed from the top, it will indicate forward movement; removed from the bottom, it will indicate backward movement. When the rectangle has its end shaved off by a diagonal line, it will indicate, depending on the end shaved and the direction of the diagonal, movement forward-right, forward- left, backward-right, and backward-left. Whether the movement is to be performed in a low, middle, or high position will be indicated by shading which moves from black through gray, parallel-lined, to white. The black rectangle indicates low or deep movement, the white rec- tangle with a dot in the center middle movement, and the diagonally- lined rectangle high movement. The two central bands in the staff are for foot positions or steps. The two outer bands are for leg gestures. The two bands directly outside the staff are for the upper body with arms, and the two beyond them for arms alone. Other symbols and the lengthening or shortening of the rectangle will indicate tempo, dynamics, and minor movements. Thus one symbol has a multiple purpose: its placement on the staff will indicate which part of the body moves, while its color, shape and size will indicate the plane in which it moves, its direction, and its speed. In addition to symbols for the major parts of the body, there are signs for all minor parts such as shoulders, fingers, face, knees, etc.

The modified Laban system has been established in America and is being taught through the Dance Notation Bureau in New York City under the direction of Ann Hutchinson, Eve Gentry, and Helen Priest.

LABILE MOVEMENT. Used particularly by Rudolf von Laban in reference to the six even-numbered swinging movements in the series of twelve swings he has developed, using the icosahedron as a framework. Labile movements are smooth, floating, gliding, or passive in character, and generally wide in dimension.

Antonym: STABILE MOVEMENT.

LATENT MOVEMENT. An imperceptible inner tension which prevents relaxed movement from becoming dead or inert.

Also, a transition which isn't expressed visually by the dancer. It may be called an inner conception of movement through which the dancer will move from A to C without performing the connecting link or transition. Franziska Boas.

In the latter respect, it is similar in its effect to percussive movement.

LEG GESTURE. Any movement made by the free leg while the weight is carried on the supporting leg.

LEGATO. 1. From the Italian, tied.

2. In music, connected; the flow from note to note without any perceptible break between the ending of one and the beginning of the next.

3. In dance, it is used for successive movements as for successive notes above.

Antonym: STACCATO.

LEVELS. See PLANES.

LOCOMOTOR MOVEMENT. Movement which progresses in space or from place to place, as distinguished from axial movement which is generally considered as movement around one or more axes in the body without progression in space. Running, skipping, and leaping are examples of locomotor movement. It is also possible to combine locomotor and axial movement, as in a turning body that also moves in space.

In general, there are eight fundamental changes of weight in moving from one place to another. They are the walk, the run, the leap, the jump, the hop, the skip, the slide, and the gallop.

LOW DANCER. One of the three types of dancer as named by Rudolf von Laban, the other two being middle and high dancer. A low dancer will be generally short and squat and will find folk movements, earth movement, or primitive movements more natural to his physique.

MECHANISTIC DANCE. Applied specifically to dance which expressed the machine, and generally to all modern dance in its early stages when it did not flow in graceful curves; a meaningless term.

MELODIC LINE. Implies movement that flows smoothly without staccato interruptions; an evenly progressing, unbroken line. The movement in melodic line will be curved movement.

Antonym: PERCUSSIVE MOVEMENT.

METAKINESIS. The psychical overtones accompanying movement; one of the four innovations of modern dance as listed by John Martin. Movement will without fail be colored by the personality of the person who produces it and will reflect his experience and temperament. Metakinesis is not different from but a part of the physical movement in the same sense that the body and the soul are two aspects of a single underlying reality. All movement is done with a purpose and is in some degree functional. It is the conscious recognition and use of this fact that distinguishes modern dance from other types.

METRIC RHYTHM. See under RHYTHM.

MIDDLE DANCER. One of the three types of dancer, as named by Rudolf von Laban, the other two being high and low dancer. A middle dancer is one who is of average height and build and who finds both aerial and earthy movements natural to his physique, although probably not to the degree that they are natural to the high or low dancer.

MIDDLE MOVEMENT. A term used to describe movements of a certain type for dance notation and other purposes:

1. In the vertical body: any arm movement at or near the horizontal plane that cuts through the shoulders and is parallel to the floor; any leg or torso movement at or near the horizontal plane that cuts through the hips and is parallel to the floor.

2. In other positions: all arm movement is considered in relation to the torso; all leg movement is considered in relation to the vertical body, as, for example, the legs are considered middle in a sitting posi· tion where the torso and legs constitute a right angle; any step with the legs straight and the foot flat is middle.

3. Note: We might consider the torso as a spool, the two ends being the horizontal planes through the shoulders and hips. These two ends or planes always remain in their same relationship to the connecting tube in no matter what position the body may be tilting or bending; thus the dimensions of the arm and leg movements may be immediately placed. The torso, however, is always considered in relation to an imaginary vertical line or to the complete vertical body.

MIME. One who apes or imitates. The term should not be confused with pantomime which imitates all sorts of actions and characters without speaking. The only type of dance to which this term as an adjective might apply is the dance to the spoken word or poetry, where the movement is reinforced by the word and may therefore be called mimic.

Further clarification may be found under DRAMATIC DANCE, PANTO-MIMIC DANCE.

MODERN DANCE. The foundations of the modern dance were established inspirationally and theoretically by Isadora Duncan who returned to natural movements and rhythms and stated the dynamic principle upon which later modern dance was to be based. In America, it was kept going by Ruth St. Denis and Ted Shawn in the Denishawn School which inspired young dancers, introduced them to many varieties and styles of movement, and made an attempt to find form through music-visualization. It was finally given a workable technique and a formal structure by Rudolf von Laban and Mary Wigman in Ger many, and by Martha Graham, Doris Humphrey, and Charles Weidman, all former members of the Denishawn School, in America.

Theoretically, the modern dance is based on dynamism; on what Bergson calls "contradictory concepts"; on the collision of two opposites such as contraction and release, fall and recovery, tension and relaxation, etc., which were formulated from natural rhythms, originally used literally, such as the breath rhythm, the wave rhythm, folding and unfolding, etc.

Technically, movement is regarded as the substance of the dance and the body is the instrument. All movement is conceived as coming from a central source (see center of movement) thereby bringing in the torso as the controlling force and abandoning movement from the joints. Movement from a central dynamo of power implies functional movement and movement which contains emotional overtones of meaning. See METAKINESIS.

Time, space, dynamism, and metakineses are the factors around which dance designs are built. The raw material of the modern dance is bodily movement and rest, based upon natural rhythms. Time is acknowledged through tempo, duration, acceleration, and retarda· tion of movement. Space is acknowledged through the three basic spatial planes: the horizontal, the vertical, the third-dimensional, and the various diagonals. Of the two elements, space and time, space has received less conscious consideration in America than in Germany. See SPACE, GERMAN DANCE.

The purpose of this bodily movement is to give expression to all emotions and mental attitudes that can be adequately expressed through movement. The subjection of this movement to preliminary selection and organization, prescribed steps, techniques, and exercises, is the primary artistic medium of the modern dance. Although no systematization has as yet been given to the modern dance which can correspond to the rigid codification of the classical ballet, there is nevertheless a natural rhythm composed of two extremes which serves as the basis of all individual techniques within the modern movement, Mary Wigman's tension-relaxation, Doris Humphrey's fall-recovery, Martha Graham's contraction-release, etc. When a universal system has fused the individual systems of the originators of modern dance, the modern dance will have become as firmly entrenched and as widely accepted as the ballet is at present.

"All additions to the pure dance should, at least ideally, enrich the art of the dance, although the more ambitious the combinations attempted and the greater the resultant complexity, the harder it is to achieve artistic unity." Note 58. These additions include music, pantomime, costumes, and stage setting. Inasmuch as the main material is bodily movement, music must always remain complementary and secondary. Wherever possible, it should be composed for the dance. See MUSIC, USES OF. Pantomime should be "a natural extension of expressive bodily motion into the realm of imitation or mimicry. The basic requirement from the point of view of the dance is that all pantomimic action should be rigorously disciplined by the rhythm and motifs of the dance itself. Pantomime cannot simply be added; the movements of the dance must take on pantomimic quality without loss of the dynamic rhythm of the dance itself." Note 59. See KINETIC PANTOMIME.

"When the dance makes use of costume and of the several arts and crafts other than acting, which pertain to the synthetic art of the theater, it does not combine with a major art, as in the case of the accompanied dance, nor does it merely extend the scope of its own proper medium as in the case of the pantomimic dance. It now calls to its aid various minor arts whose role must remain subsidiary. Whenever these arts acquire ascendancy the result is not a dance in the true sense but rather a 'spectacle' with dances introduced as diversions or interludes." Note 60.

The structural ingredient of the modern dance is the movement-phrase, a combination of movements with a beginning, a middle, and an end. The movement-phrase is only rarely a unitary artistic idea; that is, it is rarely presented only once in a dance composition. See BROKEN FORM. As in western music, so in modern dance the movement-phrase is usually repeated. It may be reiterative, repeated without change, or developmental repeated with variation.

Compositional patterns are still in the stage of experimentation. The only person in the field capable at present of giving them some definition is Doris Humphrey. The modern dance was given emotional impetus by Isadora Duncan and a certain theatrical quality by the Denishawns. The first American efforts toward formal composition took the form of music-visualization. Compositions evolved directly through movement did not emerge in America until after 1925 when Martha Graham, Doris Humphrey, and Charles Weidman left the Denishawn School and began careers as independent artists.

Of extraordinary importance for the development of composition is a system of dance notation whereby dances may be recorded so that each new dancer need not rely upon memory alone. In this respect, the Laban dance script or some variation of it should have as important results for the modern dance as a uniform system of notation had earlier for music. Such a system, universally used, would make available a library of dances upon which other dancers could build. It would also provide a solid historical basis for the dance by removing its ephemeral quality. "It is certain that until the primary medium of the dance has been organized in a manner comparable to the organization of the musical medium, and until a dance script and an accurate terminology have been devised and widely accepted, we cannot expect the musically unaccompanied dance, or indeed the dance in any of its forms, to develop into as artistically expressive a vehicle as pure music." Note 61.

See also ABSOLUTE DANCE, ABSTRACT DANCE, ART-DANCE, FREE DANCE, EXPRESSIONISTIC DANCE.

MOTION CHOIR. Term used in Germany to denote a group of lay dancers performing; distinguished from "concert group," which is a group of professional dancers. Also called movement-choir, or dance-choir.

"This method presents a new form of group experience for which performers may train individually. The self-realization achieved by the concerted activity of a group, the expression of a common idea, the exhibition of individual skill and ability for creative expression — all these are natural outcomes of movement-choirs. This new kind of dancing was evolved from gymnastics and introduced by Rudolf von Laban. Amplified effects follow the performance of the same movement in concert — in unison — in choir. . . The composite effect of the movement-choir is essentially the same as orchestration is to musical composition. The roles of the different instruments are taken over by dancers, representing different types of dancing. Of course, concerted movement by dancers is not new. The moving plastique of Dalcroze

Eurhythmics is an example in a related field, in which several individuals move in unison and identically in direction. . . . The Laban movement-choir is distinctive in its emphasis on identical movements of several dancers, not to form patterns like ballet, or merely to express rhythms, like Dalcroze Eurhythmics, but to express emotions. The movement-choir is thus nearer to the primitive dances of savages in its efforts to portray the inner man; on the other hand it is closer to ballet in its striving for grace; and finally it is reflective of Dalcroze in its use of the whole body to express rhythms." Note 62.

See also MUSIC-VISUALIZATION.

MOTOR MEMORY. Martha Graham believes "that motor memory inhabits the nervous system. . . Something she read in Plato led her to the conclusion that mythology was the psychology of another age. She wanted to go back through motor memory to the ancestral moods to find an explanation of what we are today. She uses the symbols of mythology as ancestors of present-day moods." Note 63.

See also KINESTHESIA.

MOTOR PHRASE. "The dynamic breath rhythm of the body which determines the length and timing of the movement phrase. It is opposed to the more arbitrary metrical phrase of music." Gertrude Lippincott.

See also BREATH RHYTHM, SPEECH PHRASE.

The term is also used as a synonym for MOVEMENT-PHRASE.

MOVEMENT. 1. The fundamental language of the modern dance is movement; any number of other factors may be present, but this is basic. The distinction between the modern dance and the classic ballet can not be as sharply made now as it could have been in the 1920's and 1930's. Nevertheless, such a comparison may clarify what the modern dancer means by movement. It is considered by him to be the building material from which the entire structure of the dance emerges. In this sense, all movement is considered to have a beginning, a development, and an end, with the development being given the greatest importance. In the classic ballet, the end of the movement was stressed and this was less a movement than a pose or attitude. Instead of eliding the movement between attitudes, the modern dancer presents it in its duration. The movements thus become developmental, both within themselves and in relation to preceding and succeeding movements. As C. E. Bergson has remarked, "But for us, conscious beings, it is the units that matter, for we do not count extremities of intervals, we feel and live the intervals themselves."

2. This movement is always accompanied by metakinesis. Movement refers to that which is both kinetic and metakinetic; motion refers to that which is purely or largely kinetic. Movement is a purposeful change of weight or position and is always connected by underflowing streams with a central dynamo of power. A leg motion evolved by lever-action from the pelvic girdle may become a leg movement in the modern dance when seen and felt as the culmination of a stream of movement referrable to a central motor source. Movement of any part of the body comes from the body as a whole; it has function and also overtones of meaning and emotion.

3 "Doris Humphrey has called movement the arc between two deaths. Thus, movement is essentially unbalance, and the degree of unbalance conditions the intensity of the movement. That is, the amount of distortion of a movement determines its tension. Rhythm is the result of the organization of these parts, these tension-stages, into a unified whole." Note 64.

MOVEMENT-CHOIR. See MOTION CHOIR.

MOVEMENT-PHRASE. A grouping of movements; "a succession of movements from a common impulse, not necessarily sufficient to constitute a complete statement of action but containing either the introduction of a theme or a response to such a theme already introduced. . . The series of movements would necessarily have a characteristic pulse, though they need not inevitably be evenly spaced or timed, and would possess a unity that set them apart from what had been done previously or what was to follow." Note 65.

In music, a phrase is a regular and symmetrical course of notes which begin and complete the intended expression. It "is one of the smallest among the divisions which distinguish the form of a musical work. Where there are distinct portions marked off by closes like full stops, and half closes like stops of less emphasis, the complete divisions are generally called periods, and the lesser divisions phrases. The word is not and can hardly be used with much exactness and uniformity, for sometimes a phrase may be all, as it were, contained in one breath, and sometimes subordinate divisions may be very clearly marked." Note 66.

Inasmuch as the term "period" is sometimes used in modern dance to express the same thing as the term "movement-phrase," the terms may lead to some ambiguity in the dance as they do in music. If both are to be used, it may be stated in general that a phrase is shorter than a period.

See also ACTION-MODE, PATTERN.

MUSIC, USES OF. Music may be used by the modern dancer solely as a contrapuntal background for movement. It may be used only to mark the tempo and phrasing, with no consideration of the meaning or value of the music per se. Such use alters the music at will to fit the immediate needs of the dancer; it is an arbitrary method, to be condemned. The subject or mood of the music may be reinterpreted by movement, in which case the music is considered programmatic, whether actually so or not. This is usually a slipshod, hyper-romantic method, re-expressing what has already been adequately expressed. Music may be visualized in a literal sense by movement. See MUSIC-VISUALIZATION. Most important, however, is the use of music written in conjunction with the development of the dance and thus an integral part of the dance composition. The less intrusive the music is as an independent element, the better its coordination with the composition in movement will be.

"The actual process of composing dance accompaniments is based entirely upon practical experience and work. It is not possible to give a precise formula for composing dance music as one would outline the form of a sonata or fugue. We must realize that the most direct means of achieving a vital fusion of music and the dance is to create music especially to complement the form of the dance and complete its inner intention. Each new dance creates its own form. In this way the lines of direction for the composition are drawn from the dance itself. The dance music of the future will no longer assert its motive, then proceed on an entirely independent line to develop the direction of already existing musical forms, even those such as the minuet and the gavotte." Note 67.

The development of music strictly for the dance is greatly indebted to the experiments of Mary Wigman. "In her treatment of music, Wigman has again been completely radical. . . . Her first dance was, as a matter of interest, without music of any sort, and frequently since then she has omitted all sound from the accompaniment of some of her compositions and of particular sections of others. With a realization of the fact that the dancer's music is essentially his own song with the percussive accents of his bodily rhythms, she has evolved the ideal type of dance accompaniment. Her music, composed either along with the creation of her dance or after the dance has been completed, is of greatest simplicity and frequently has no independent musical validity whatever apart from the dance. It employs almost exclusively nonorchestral instruments, matching the quality of the dance's tone with melodies on unsophisticated flutes, gongs, drums. The employment at times of the inappropriate and unadaptable piano, which practical necessity makes apparently unavoidable for the dancer, is the only exception to her complete musical logic." Note 68.

Wigman has remarked: "Though I have always had a strong feeling for music it seemed from the very start most natural for me to express my own nature by means of pure movement. After years of trial I have come to realize in a very final way, that for me the creation of a dance to music already written cannot be complete and satisfactory. But while music easily evokes in me a dance reaction, it is in the development of the dance that a great divergence so often occurs. For usually a dance idea, a theme, however inspired, by a state of feeling, or indirectly by music, sets up independent reactions. The theme calls for its own development. It is in working this out that I find my dance parting company with the music. The parallel development of the dance with the already completely worked out musical idea is what I find in most instances to be functionally wrong. Each dance demands organic autonomy." Note 69.

MUSIC-VISUALIZATION. One of the first efforts on the part of dancers to find a formal structure for the modern dance. It received its name in the Denishawn School of the Dance and is largely associated with certain compositions of Ruth St. Denis, with and without the assistance of the young Doris Humphrey. It was not an innovation on the part of St. Denis but was rather an adaptation, with few changes, of Dalcroze's Eurhythmics. "The idea of a 'synchoric orchestra' in which each of some fifty or sixty dancers was to represent a particular instrument, whether actually to orchestral accompaniment or not, was actually a

Dalcrozean practice. Later, there was some specific teaching of the Dalcroze method by Elsa Findlay in the school." Note 70.

A full description of the method was written in 1925 by Ruth St. Denis for the Denishawn Magazine in which she said, "Music Visualization in its purest form is the scientific translation into bodily action of the rhythmic, melodic and harmonic structure of a musical composition, without intention to in any way interpret or reveal any hidden meaning apprehended by the dancer. First let me explain that I coined this phrase 'Music Visualization' some years ago in our school in Los Angeles, in order to avoid the much abused word 'interpretive' as applied to dancing. . . . The result of my meditations was the conception of my Synchoric Orchestra, and, from the principles involved therein, the whole series of our music visualizations, from the Bach Inventions which Mr. Shawn visualized and which the Concert Dancers used, for two seasons, down to the Schutt Suite for Violin and Piano, which is new on this season's program. In a two-part Invention, two separate groups dance, each group moving to the notes of its own part only, and remaining still on the rests in that part. Dancing at the same time, the two groups imprint upon the eye a correlative image to the one given to the ear by the playing of this two-part Invention on the piano, that of two themes, each distinct in itself, harmoniously mingling to produce a charming and perfect structural whole. In other compositions, such as Beethoven's Sonata called the Pathetique there is obviously an emotional coloring. After the abstract emotional coloring is decided upon, it must be kept in mind as influencing the quality of the gesture used throughout by the dancers. The time in which the music is written must be recognized, and the rhythmic pattern apprehended. Then each note must have its correlative translation; an eighth note has a definite length, and its visualization must be a movement exactly as long. Dynamics must be considered. A softly struck note should be moved softly and with economy of force, while a crashing chord must be visualized with more physical energy. The rise and fall of the melody should have some answer in the rise and fall of the body above the plane of the stage, the position of the notes on the printed staff being in some degree analagous to the range of posture the body can control from lying flat on the stage to the highest leap above the floor. There is sometimes a wide variety of movements that can be used equally well to visualize certain elements in the music, and here is where the selective quality of the artist comes into play. A trill in the music may be visualized as a whirl, or a vibration throughout the body accented in the arms and hands, or a ballet emboit, for instance. . . If one is visualizing an abstract composition, sonata, concerto, or etude, obviously the quality of the gesture should be kept abstract, should avoid a definite school, national or racial style,—it should be universal gesture.

"All of these rules are used as bases to start from. Often we depart from them ourselves for many reasons. In designing dances for entertainment purposes, the fact is borne in upon the creator that the public will stand for abstract movement only in small doses. And so, upon a sound base of rendering the value of the notes of the music into a corresponding value of movement, there is superimposed a surface idea to trick the eye of those beholders who have neither the interest nor the training to apprehend the actual visualization principles which are being applied and actually worked out in the dance which he sees. Thus in Mr. Shawn's visualization of the Revolutionary Etude of Chopin, he has superimposed a dramatic narrative, while at the same time the composition is visualized on rigid principles. His gesture enacting the story of the crazed revolutionist exactly parallels the melodic theme, while the whirling figures behind him symbolizing flame and fury, visualize the accompaniment.

" . . . I feel . . . that parallel to our studies of music visualization should be the study of the dance as an independent art, with no music accompaniment at all. At the time I first began active creating along Music Visualization lines, Miss Doris Humphrey, who had been in my company for several seasons, was closely associated with me. Through these years she has collaborated with me on many compositions, and of late years has independently visualized along the principles I had worked out, many beautiful numbers."

"One experience which led me to this resolve to analyze and to arrive at fundamental truths about the relation of dance and music, was the performance of one of our music dancers purporting to interpret a symphony. I heard a large symphony orchestra playing one of the well-known symphonic works. I saw a woman moving about the stage in, at times, a rhythmic, and at other times, a dramatic manner, which had in it much depth of feeling, much nobility of movement and much pure beauty of bodily line, but which had almost no connection with the musical composition to which she was dancing. That this dancer was trying to express through her movements the spirit of the work was quite evident, but in actual fact she could give but a few gestures, a few pregnant pauses, that in any way visualized, much less interpreted, the great symphonic work whose harmonies and dynamics were floating about her. I went home from this performance very thoughtful, for the motives of her performance found a most profound agreement with my own." Note 71.

This method is an inadequate approach to dance form, partly because music does not work spatially in the same sense as does the dance, and partly because it imposes an alien rhythm on the natural physical rhythms of the body. The method, nevertheless, had a profound influence upon such dancers as Doris Humphrey. It was not abandoned by the modern dancer until each, in his own way, had discovered that movement was the substance of the dance.

It is of interest that music-visualization should have come into favor in the ballet in the 1930's and 1940's in the choreography of Leonide Massine and George Balanchine at the time that it was being abandoned by the modern dance. This manifestation of it is called symphonic ballet, but its methods are the same as those employed by St. Denis. The dance rhythm is based upon the music, following it beat by beat and measure by measure, at the same time that it endeavors to visualize the theme and moods in choreographic terms. The dance and the music are correlated and made to complement each other. The choreography follows the melody, the emotional quality, and the change of key in the musical composition.

NARROW. Denotes the condition of a movement which is neither straight nor angular, but gently curved, as the arms curved over the head in ballet, or, a slightly bent leg.

Antonym: WIDE.

NATURAL DANCE. 1. Dance that employs the natural movements of the body, such as walking, running, etc.

2. The term was at one time employed in educational practice. Natural movements were used in order to give the dancer control over his body and to make it an expressive medium. Expression thus superseded form in importance. The term should not be confused with nature dancing. See also BODY CORRECTIVES, HEALTH DANCING.

3. The words "nature" and "natural" were frequently used by Isadora Duncan who was reacting against the codification of the classical ballet. She has said, "Then when I opened the door to nature again, revealing a different kind of dance, some people explained it all by saying, 'See, it is natural dancing.' But with its freedom, its accordance with natural movement, there was always design too, even in nature you find sure, even rigid design. 'Natural' dancing should mean only that the dance never goes against nature, not that anything is left to chance. Nature must be the source of all art, and dance must make use of nature's forces in harmony and rhythm, but the dancer's movement will always be separate from any movement in nature." Note 72. This statement, made about 1909, was partly instigated by the growth of a variety of dance-styles based on natural movement that were formless and inchoate. Although natural movements and natural rhythms were to remain part of the new dance that reacted against the ballet, the term "natural dance" was quickly dropped and the term "modern dance" took its place.

NATURAL MOVEMENT. 1. Generally, movement derived from some natural source and recognizable as such. Not to be confused with pantomimic movement, which copies or imitates specific gestures, usually for burlesque or satiric purposes.

2. Under the heading of natural movement belong the movements used in expressing natural rhythms, such as folding-unfolding, opening-closing, rising-falling, pressing-pulling, bending-reaching, etc.

3. Also the so-called transitional movements, or those which convey the body from place to place, such as the step, walk, run, jump, hop, leap, gallop, slide, and skip, all of which are a variation on the simple step or transfer of weight.

4. Also types of rhythmic movement such as rotating, twisting, turning, undulating, heaving, swinging, swaying, vibrating, bending, stretching, beating, and shaking.

NATURAL RHYTHMS. Under this heading belong physical rhythms and all other rhythms observed in nature.

1. Of physical rhythms, those most commonly observed are the breath-rhythm and the heart beat. The latter is often mentioned in treatment of this subject but has had little observable effect on the dance as a guiding or controlling element. The breath-rhythm, on the

other hand, has been consciously used and was the element most commonly noted in early forms of the modern dance, such as aesthetic dancing, natural dancing, the Duncan dance, etc. For further treatment of this, see under breath-rhythm.

2. Of nature rhythms, that most commonly referred to and most gen· erally used in the early modern dance was folding-unfolding. That stressed by Isadora Duncan was the wave rhythm. Other types of this dual nature are:

a. closing-opening, which is one form of the folding-unfolding principle;

b. rise-fall, partially derived from the wave rhythm and another form of the folding-unfolding principle;

c. press-pull, a variety of the principle of attraction and repulsion; and

d. bending-reaching, a soft cradling movement.

3. All rhythms of this nature, with the sole exception of the purely physical breath-rhythm, have been excessively colored with emotion and belong more strictly to the so-called romantic dance than to the modern dance which eventually grew from it. Movement based on these rhythms is largely derivative, imitative, and panders more to the weak, sentimental dancer. Despite this criticism, these rhythms have nevertheless been the forerunners of the modern movement and must be remembered as such.

NATURE DANCE. A type of dance no longer seriously practiced except for very small children. It may have grown from Delsarte who made an intensive study of pantomimic gesture. The movements in the nature dance were strongly pantomimic and were linked together on the thread of an innocuous story usually depicting young girls cavorting in the midst of nature.

Not to be confused with natural dancing.

NEO-GRECIAN DANCE. Term suggested by Elizabeth Selden to replace Greek dance inasmuch as little is actually known about the dancing of the Greeks. The neo-Grecian dance is a reconstruction of the Greek dance based on scant evidence. Interest in this goes back to the later nineteenth and early twentieth centuries when Delsarte and others influenced by him attempted to build a structure on the attitudes of Greek sculpture and vase painting. This kind of reconstruction is quite different from the approach of Isadora Duncan who was concerned with discovering the principle upon which Greek gesture was based. She was not interested in composing a dance by the addition of a series of gestures and attitudes copied from Greek art. She herself scorned the vapid dancing that went by the name of Greek during her life. Nevertheless, these groups, through their use of a softer and more flowing movement, opened the way for the discovery of movement as the substance of the dance.

See also DUNCAN DANCE, DUNCAN THEORY.

NEW DANCE. A name given in the 1920's to that dance which turned against the classic ballet and which is now called modern dance. The term was rarely used in America but was used in Germany to denote the work of Mary Wigman, Rudolf von Laban, and others in the Central European school.

OPEN MOVEMENT. Refers to movement whose path is away from the body and implies crescendo. Open moment involves the act of motion in an increasing spatial area, whereas peripheral movement, with which it is likely to be confused, involves the act of motion at the periphery. The former goes toward the periphery; the latter occurs at the periphery.

Centrifugal movement denotes movement impelled outward with the emphasis on rotation and may be considered to be a kind of open movement.

Antonym: CLOSED MOVEMENT.

OPPOSITION. 1. The opposition of different parts of the body is the instinctive method by which the body maintains equilibrium. For example, in a walk, the left arm moves forward with the right leg, balancing on the one side of the body the weight displaced forward on the other. If the walk is done with both arms hanging at the sides, a noticeable strain will result because of the additional strain being placed upon the legs to preserve balance.

2. Opposition refers to the opposite direction of any two dominant lines in a posture or an attitude; or to the opposite direction of any two dominant lines formed by two or more bodies, as: one figure lying on the ground and one figure erect with the feet behind the

recumbent figure's head, the two lines forming a right angle. All such designs are considered as seen from the audience, inasmuch as an opposition viewed from one position may become a unison when seen from another position. For example, a figure seated on the floor with the arms following the right angle constituted by torso and legs will be an opposition when viewed from the side but will become a unison when viewed from the front. See also succession. Doris Humphrey

3. Opposition is sometimes used as synonymous with contrapposto, a term used by Italian sculptors of the late Renaissance to denote a twisting or spiral movement of the body. When the term is used in this sense in reference to ballet, it is misleading since such opposition of the upper and lower body is not consciously so used in the ballet. The term "simple opposition" is suggested to indicate the simple alternation of opposite arm and leg in a single plane, as in walking, running, etc., and the term contrapposto for an opposition which involves a twisting of the torso and not merely a counterbalance of members.

OPPOSITIONAL TENSION. That quality which gives vitality to a movement. "Some degree of opposition must be in force constantly, as: if a dancer tilts somewhat sideward, raises the right arm side-high and the left leg side-deep and comparatively close to the body with the focus of attention in the arm, the vitality of the arm movement, which stretches upward, will be preserved and increased by a contrasting downward pull through the opposite leg." Helen Tamiris. It is the pulling of these members in opposite directions — oppositional tension — that gives life to the movement, creating a resistance to the main direction and thereby intensifying it.

See also RESISTANCE, STATIC TENSION, SUSPENSION, SUSTAINED MOVEMENT, and TILT, to which in some degree this principle is applicable.

ORTHOGRAPHY. Commonly, the art or practice of writing words with the proper letters, according to common usage. In dance, the art or practice of writing down movements on paper with the proper signs and symbols. The signs and symbols so used are called dance script.

PANTOMIMIC DANCE. A dramatic representation in which the dancers, enacting various characters, express their meaning through movement without dialogue. The pantomimic dance is the closest of all dance forms to the spoken drama and utilizes the general framework of the drama such as characters, well-defined plot of events, acts and scenes, specific costumes, and scenery.

When less specific in subject matter, using ideas instead of events, this type of dance is called dramatic dance.

Antonym: ABSTRACT DANCE.

PANTOMIMIC MOVEMENT. Any movement contrived to ape or imitate some generally known movement, character, or event, usually for satiric purposes. Pantomimic movement is specific and concrete. Such movement used in a dance composition is, or should be, subject to the rhythmic laws of that composition. Because of the interpolation of pantomimic movement into abstract dances without recognition of these laws, and because of the unfused mingling of pantomime and pure dance in many ballets, the term "pantomimic movement" is in itself not absolutely clear. Charles Weidman suggests the term kinetic pantomime to define any such imitative movement used in a dance composition.

PARALLELISM. The movement of two or more parts of the body in the same direction at the same time.

PASSIVE ACTION. A term used by Elizabeth Selden to denote a combination of movements that have dispensed with tension, visibly, at least, and have the quality of quietness and dreaminess. The feeling of controlled direction, which will be implicit in all movement that approaches the tension-pole, is here absent. The term is somewhat vague.

See also ENERGIZED ACTION.

PASSIVE MOVEMENT. That type of movement which seems to be impelled by its own momentum, or in which the driving power is not consciously made evident.

Antonym: ACTIVE MOVEMENT.

PATH. The lines described by the movements of the body or any of its parts through space. The path of the feet is more generally known as the floor-pattern.

Abstract designs created by Pablo Picasso in the air with the aid of a light and photographed by Gjon Mili are of interest to the dancer in that the designs occupying time are frozen by the photographer in a single image. The leg and arm movements of the dancer describe similar paths in the air during a dance. Inasmuch as the complete path, because of the time taken to trace it, will be only a memory image, its duration should be reasonably short or its beginning will be forgotten.

PATTERN. A series of movements conceived as an entity and capable of being so perceived by the spectator. Obviously, the series cannot be too long or its quality of wholeness will be lost.

Synonymous with movement-phrase, which is the preferred term, since pattern has other connotations, such as a model prepared for imitation, an exemplar, an ornamental design.

PAUSE. Any moment in the dance where no directional movement occurs; synonymous with "rest" in music. Also used in dance notation to indicate any point where the movement of one member of the body is held while some other member performs a movement or gesture.

"Just as a musical rest is not mere silence, but silence impregnated with artistic significance by a surrounding pattern of musical tones, so, in the dance, what is sheer absence of movement at the level of the raw material can become, in conjunction with bodily movement, profoundly expressive." Note 73. The pause is far more significant in modern dance than in classical ballet where, because of the stress in the latter upon the concluding attitude rather than upon the movement that leads to it, the pause becomes an abrupt cessation of movement.

PENDULAR SWINGS. A type of swing wherein the movement is as effortless as in the pendulum. The least amount of effort is involved in maintaining the movement which thus appears to be determined in its back and forth directions by the pull of gravity alone. It may or may not result in dimnishing arcs during its progress.

See also BALLISTIC SWING, SWING.

PERCUSSIVE MOVEMENT. The term may be used quite literally to indicate staccato movement. Antonym: MELODIC LINE.

Superficially similar to angular movement but differs in that angular movements have straight lines and angles as their end points, whereas percussive movements often have the unrealized curve or circle as their end points. Thus, a partial arc of a curve or circle is performed and stopped with such vigor and abruptness that it carries the spectator's eye beyond the partial arc into the complete circle. Or, the dancer imagines a 90 degree arc but performs only 45 degrees of that arc with such concentration of power as to force the spectator to complete the full 90 degrees in his mind's eye. Percussive movements may therefore be called segments of a curve or circle. Because of their brief duration, they approach the straight line. Percussive movements provide vigor and vitality to the movement in general and prevent it from dissipating itself, retaining it within a given space-cube. Martha Graham

It is most characteristic of the Graham technique. "One of her departures was in what she calls percussive movement, movement of sharp accent and rebound, as of the downbeat of bare feet at the moment of shifting weight; of the off-beat, as of the accented leaning of the body in different directions; of short, unbroken movements that look unfinished, yet complete themselves in space." Note 74. "The Graham school builds all gesture on a percussive stroke proceeding from the hips that releases movement like an after-beat through the shoulders, arms, and legs very much the way continuous action is sent the length of a whip by a single jerk of the handle, the body maintaining its balance by thrusting the hips, not outward as in ballet dancing, but forward over the bent knees which act like a spring flexing and relaxing as the hip impetus drives motion through them." Note 75.

PERIOD. See MOVEMENT-PHRASE.

PERIPHERAL MOVEMENT. 1. Movement at the circumference or outward bounds of a thing; movement farthest from the axis. In the single body, usually movement by arms or legs farthest from the torso; movement at the circumference with the trunk as focus. In a group, any movement at the sides or periphery when a focus of attention has been established in the center; or movement on one side of the stage when a focus of attention has been established on the other.

2. Similar to centripetal movement, except that peripheral movement is at the outward bounds, whereas centripetal movement goes to the outward bounds.

3. Any expansion to the periphery, as when the dancer stands with arms outspread and high and projects an invisible outward force

through the motionless arms. This movement is not visual; any posture in which the main lines are consciously felt to be projected by the dancer as outgoing is peripheral movement. Hanya Holm

Antonym: CENTRAL MOVEMENT. See also OPEN MOVEMENT.

PHRASE. Any group of movements which begin and complete the intended expression; similar to musical usage. The length is usually determined by the breath.

Movement-phrase is suggested to replace the simple term when necessary in order to avoid confusion with the musical phrase.

PHYSICAL RHYTHM. See NATURAL RHYTHMS.

PLANES. 1. Three main planes are used for simplification, although the movements of the body do not remain in these three alone.

a. The vertical plane is considered to be that which contains the frontal silhouette of the body, as: a movement by each arm from hanging position to direct side, right and left, to directly overhead will cross the vertical plane.

b. The horizontal plane is that which cuts through the hips and is parallel to the floor, and that which cuts through the shoulders and is parallel to the floor.

c. The backward-forward plane is that which cuts the body into two equal halves of right side and left side. An arm movement from hanging position to direct forward to directly over head will cross the forward part of the plane.

2. Generally, and somewhat vaguely, the stage space is sometimes considered to be composed of three parallel planes, that closest to the floor being Deep, that highest from the floor being HIGH, and that in between being Middle. However, a sitting figure may do a high movement in the deep plane so that no concise demarcation of planes can be made for the stage space.

PLASTIC DANCE. Term generally applied to early phases of modern dance to denote its use of the body as a whole with emphasis on mass, volume, plasticity, etc., as distinguished from the linear and silhouette qualities of ballet.

POINTED MOVEMENT. Any movement which is sharp, concise, and clearly articulated. The movement need not necessarily be angular.

POSITIONS. The five positions of the feet, developed in classical ballet, have been taken over or adapted by certain modern dancers. Those most commonly used are the 2nd and 4th positions. In the 2nd position, the feet point to the sides on a single line and are separated, usually by more than the ballet's required twelve inches. In the 4th position, the toe of one foot is ahead of and separated from the heel of the other foot; in general, the feet are not as turned out as in ballet.

POSTURE. According to Martha Graham, "posture is dynamic, not static. It is a self-portrait of being. It is psychological as well as physiological. I use the word 'posture' to mean that instant of seeming stillness when the body is poised for most intense, most subtle action, the body at its moment of greatest potential efficiency. The nearest to the norm, as it has been observed and practiced over centuries, has been the ear in line perpendicularly with the shoulder, the shoulder with the pelvic bone, the pelvic bone in line with the arch of the foot." Note 76

PULSE. Generally, a regular beating or throbbing; a wave or spurt. In dance, it refers to that point where the movement is initiated. Helen Tamiris

RALLENTANDO. Decrease in time, as distinguished from decrescendo which is a decrease in force.

Synonym: RITARDANDO; antonym: ACCELERANDO.

READINESS. See CONTROLLED RELAXATION.

RECITAL. See DANCE RECITAL.

RECOVERY. See under FALL-RECOVERY.

RECURRING THEME. One of the compositional forms used by modern dance. It is a movement theme which recurs throughout the dance and almost invariably in the same area on the stage, by which it is immediately identified. The transitional themes between the recurring themes are different either rhythmically or dynamically, so as to point up the recurring theme, as: a slow recurring theme may have syncopated transitions, etc. Similar in many respects to the leitmotif or distinguishing theme in opera. Doris Humphrey

RELAXATION. That period of diminished tension between two periods of tension; a relaxation of the muscles in order to prepare for a new contraction or expansion and create a new tension. "To relax only for the sake of relaxing leads to inactivity or inertia. A state of collapse is non-productive." Hanya Holm

See also TENSION-RELAXATION.

RELEASE. 1. To set free from restraint or confinement.

2. Used in a strictly physiological sense as a non-contraction, or a return to normal condition, the extreme of which is relaxation. It is used in this sense in the dance only to make way for another contraction.

3. Used in a special sense by Martha Graham in the term contraction-release; not to be confused with an abatement or remission of tension or contraction. Release is caused by a chest expansion or inhalation which gives the appearance of freedom from the previous restraint and contraction, but which is actually a replacement of front contraction by back contraction. The release of the front torso muscles may be accomplished by a relaxation, an unloosing, but such a condition would appear dead and inert. It is therefore accompanied, for dance purposes, by a contraction of the back muscles which expands or stretches the front muscles and intensifies the appearance of release.

See also DYNAMISM, TENSION-RELAXATION.

REPETITIOUS FORM. One of the compositional forms used by modern dance. The use of a single movement-phrase and its variations for an entire dance or for a section of a long group dance. It involves the shifting of accent in various ways to give new aspects to the chosen movement, and also the use of different planes, etc. It may be altered temporally, spatially, or dynamically. In a group dance, the theme may be divided among several dancers. Doris Humphrey

RESISTANCE. Used by Esther Junger as movement performed with a conscious knowledge of space and gravity. A resistance to space and gravity is consciously willed by the dancer; it gives vitality and meaning to the movement. It may also be called a consciously felt and willed tension.

See also OPPOSITIONAL TENSION, INTENSITY.

REST. See PAUSE.

RESTING AXIS. See under AXIAL MOVEMENT.

RESULTANT RHYTHM. A rhythm which is the resultant of two rhythms played simultaneously.

Illustrations: a. Two groups may perform, one on a three and one on a four, each performing different movements except at those points where the notes coincide, where they perform identical movements. This requires good stage-spacing so that the two groups may be viewed in their totality by the spectator; too great a separation would prevent the resultant rhythm from being apprehended. b. One group may perform to two rhythms in different meters, moving only on the coinciding beats. c. Three groups may perform, one on the three, one on the four, and the third only on the coinciding beats, (the resultant rhythm,) etc.

RHYTHM. "Rhythm was no longer synonymous with beat but came to mean a sequence of self-evolved movements, harmonized with the fundamental pulse and flow of the body-rhythms and capable of repetition. Movements were used only in relation to a central dynamo of motor power, which Isadora located in the chest, the seat of the two vital rhythms of the body, blood and breath. The shift in the meaning of dance was one from line to mass, from building by accretion to organic evolution." Note 77.

In reference to experimentation in contemporary music, Louis Horst has remarked: "But this experimentation away from rhythmic regularity was not only a desire for greater rhythmic freedom, it basically was really a desire for greater truth in action, a way towards a new realism. And it is this view of rhythmic experimentation in music that links it so closely to the contemporary dance's urge towards a factual and honest employment of action-rhythms — a true and new realism based on action, not attitude." In commenting upon new rhythms used in modern dance, he states that "the quintuple (5/4 or 5/8) time produces an unsymmetrical (or dissonant) rhythm sufficiently interesting to have induced the first modern composers to make experiments therein. It is the most favored for anything like continuous movement. 7/8 or 7/4 time is found more rarely. In dance, the five-rhythm is most effective when the movements occur on 1 and 4, or on 1 and 3. This ratio of 3 to 2 produces a much greater sense of rhythmic distortion than a ratio of 4 to 2, or of 3 to 1. . . In Martha Graham's Hymn to the Virgin (from Primitive Mysteries) there are several sections in 5/8 time that do not break the lyric flow of the composition. Another innovation has been effected by the use of a single-beat bar; a time signature of 1/4. The Greeks called this the monometer. In this the idea of accented and unaccented beats must be put firmly aside... This rhythm should be especially adaptable in dance for single strong movements, whether repeated or not." Note 78.

In analyzing the principle of fall and recovery, Doris Humphrey has said: "The Rhythm exercises specify the duality, the conflict which is the basis of rhythmic movement: fall and recovery, which visualizes the two poles, at each of which the motion might cease... The initial emphasis is on feeling, on the definitely receptive reaction of the body to the particular movement. When the body is not repeating it mechanically by rote, but has accepted it and has complete control of it, then the 'count' is analyzed and learned; and following this, accent. To make a bridge between the two, the accent may be placed at first in a simple routine order, coinciding with the strongest body movement. Later it may be shifted to the weaker movement, preceding or following the strong movement. By becoming an off-accent, it increases the student's feeling of the body and also increases the strength of the strong movement, which has to depend on itself alone for accent." Note 79.

Humphrey makes a distinction between meter and rhythm by referring to metric rhythm or motor rhythm for the first and breath rhythm for the second. See SPEECH PHRASE. In this connection, H. W. Fowler's definition of rhythm in speech is completely applicable also to the dance. "Rhythmless speech or writing," he states, "is like the flow of liquid from a pipe or tap; it runs with smooth monotony from when it is turned on to when it is turned off, provided it is clear stuff; if it is turbid, the smooth flow is queerly and abruptly checked from time to time, and then resumed. Rhythmic speech or writing is like the waves of the sea, moving onward with alternate rise and fall, connected yet separate, like but different, suggestive of some law, too complex for analysis or statement, controlling the relations between wave and wave, waves and sea, phrase and phrase, phrases and speech. Rhythm is not a matter of counting syllables and measuring the distance between accents. It does mean so arranging the parts of your whole that each shall enhance, or at least not detract from, the general effect upon the ear. Metre is measurement, rhythm is flow, a flow with pulsations as infinitely various as the shape and size and speed of the waves; and infinite variety is not amenable to tabulation such as can be applied to metre." Note 80.

After Isadora Duncan, but considerably before the modern dance had arrived at a formal structure, Dalcroze had stated that "by means of movement of the whole body, we may equip ourselves to realise and perceive rhythms. This consciousness of rhythm is required by means of muscular contractions and relaxations in every degree of strength and rapidity." Note 81.

RHYTHMIC DANCE. The term was used in the period immediately preceding the advent of the modern dance. Rhythmic dance had as its aim the emphasis on rhythmic quality above all else. The term is vague and is used without precision. It may apply to types of natural dancing, the neo-Grecian dance, or the Duncan dance. It has been used by Elizabeth Selden to refer less to a type of dance than to a technique of movement which she finds as the basis of all aspects of the modern dance.

It may be applied to the dance that followed Isadora Duncan up to the point where it became systematized in the work of Wigman, Humphrey, Graham, Holm, Weidman, and others. It was useful to describe the difference between the new dance and ballet, but is no longer in common usage.

RITARDANDO. Decrease in time, as distinguished from decrescendo which is a decrease in force.

Synonym: RALLENTANDO. Antonym: ACCELERANDO.

ROMANTIC DANCE. The revolutionary work of Isadora Duncan, Ruth St. Denis and others in the early twentieth century. The expression of emotional experience was considered of such importance that it led to the abandonment of formalism. Having not as yet evolved a technique of movement based upon its own premises, the romantic dancer borrowed movements from many sources, including the Greek and the oriental. These might be woven together by pantomimic gesture and certain ballet steps and attitudes. Formal structure awaited the arrival of a new generation of dancers in Germany and America.

See also DUNCAN DANCE.

RONDO. In dance, it refers to the recurrence of a movement-phrase or series of movement-phrases at stated intervals during the development of the dance. It is similar to the recurrence of a chorus in a song. Martha Graham used the rondo form in her solo composition, Frontier.

In music, "a piece of music having one principal subject, to which a return is always made after the introduction of other matter, so as to give a symmetrical or rounded form to the whole." Note 82.

SCHRIFTTANZ. The method of dance notation devised by Rudolf von Laban; see LABAN DANCE NOTATION. Also called KINETOGRAPHIE LABAN.

SELECTIVE FORM. Term proposed to replace "distortion" or "distorted movement," these being misinterpreted by many. Selective form refers to all movements used for expressive purposes; these are all in some degree removed from the everyday, natural movement and in this sense distorted or abstracted.

The selection of a few indicative movements from a welter of possible natural movements, and their lengthening, accentuation, intensification, etc., for the purposes of expression constitute selective form Doris Humphrey

SEQUENTIAL MOVEMENT. Self-evolving movement used by the modern dance; movement of an entire dance or section of a dance sustained, each movement growing from the other; movement not arbitrarily selected but organic, based on natural rhythms. It is suggested to replace the term "continuous movement."

Although not named by Isadora Duncan, nevertheless sequential movement was the basis of all her compositions. She said, in 1902-03: "The expression of the modern school of ballet, wherein each action is an end; and no movement, pose or rhythm is successive or can be made to evolve succeeding action, is an expression of degeneration, of living death. All the movements of our modern ballet school are sterile movements because they are unnatural. The primary or fundamental movements of the new school of the dance must have within them the seeds from which will evolve all other movements, each in turn to give birth to others in unending sequence of still higher and greater expression, thoughts and ideas." Note 83. At a later time, she remarked: "Every movement, even in repose, contains the quality of fecundity, possesses the power to give birth to another movement."

Note 84. "The Greeks understood the continuing beauty of a movement that mounted, that spread, that ended with a promise of re-birth. The true dancer starts with one slow movement and mounts from that gradually, following the rising curve of his inspiration, up to those gestures that exteriorize his fullness of feeling, spreading ever wider the impulse that has swayed him, fixing it in another expression." Note 85. "True movements, moreover, are not invented; they are discovered." Note 86.

Similar beliefs have been voiced by Mary Wigman. ". . . the fundamental idea of any creation arises in me or, rather, out of me as a completely independent dance theme. This theme, however primitive or obscure at first, already contains its own development and alone dictates its singular and logical sequence." Note 87.

SILENT DANCE. See DANCE WITHOUT MUSIC.

SONG-FORM. One of the simplest compositional forms in the modern dance. It may be a composition of two different movement-themes A and B or two different themes concluding with a repetition of the first A, B, A. In the latter respect, song-form is synonymous with ABA form or folk form.

SPACE. Inasmuch as space may refer to a two-dimensional interval between two things, such as the space left between words, or to a three-dimensional cube, capable of almost unlimited expansion or compression, it becomes necessary to define the manner in which it is used by the modern dancer. For him, it will denote always a three-dimensional cube. The classic ballet worked almost entirely in line (graphic linear pattern) with movement presented on a flat frontal plane in silhouette against a more or less realistic backdrop. In this sense, its composition was identical with that developed by the Italian Renaissance painter who, in general, used a band of figures in the background and a backdrop of interior architecture, exterior architecture, or landscape in the background, both kept parallel to the picture plane. The middle ground was suggested mainly by shading and served only as a brief and inactive bridge between foreground and background. The modern dancer, through his space-consciousness, is belatedly employing devices to activate space in depth which had already been indicated in painting in the 17th century.

The modern dance works in a cube of space and so controls its movement as to determine the size of the cube, which may be a small one containing the single body, as through centripetal movement, a large one containing the single body, as through centrifugal movement, and innumerable variations of these for the single body and the group. The size of the cube may be extended or diminished within a single dance, depending upon the character of the movement. The space may be actually delimited by the movement to cubes within the volume of the stage-cube, or, by carefully controlled movement, it may be extended indefinitely.

"Spatial problems have been treated most cavalierly by composers in general; it has frequently been thought quite enough to keep the face toward the audience and to balance a sortie to the right with a sortie to the left. Instinctively the better composers have discovered other and more respectable devices from time to time, but not until the advent of Rudolf von Laban with his theory, and more particularly Mary Wigman with her incomparable practice, was the subject of space given the attention it deserves. By the dancer's prevailing awareness of the space in which and through which he moves, he relates himself consciously and visibly to his environment, and not only to the physical aspects of that environment but also to its emotional overtones. He places himself, as it were, in his universe, recognizing the existence of outside forces, benign and hostile. The dancer, on the other hand, who lacks this consciousness of the immediate world that surrounds him must necessarily concentrate on the exploitation of his person and his skills." Note 88.

Spatial problems, it must be borne in mind, may have many manifestations. The fact that the German dance treats space differently from the American dance and makes its presence more acutely felt does not necessarily mean that the American dance ignores space. To the German dancer it is an enveloping fluid of infinite dimensions; it already exists and his dance is an acceptance of it, a conflict with it, or a surrender to it. The American dancer, on the other hand, either accepts the cubical space of the stage or builds the varying spatial cubes during the dance. Such space is always clear and limpid; it never conveys the sense of an antagonist. This difference has been felt by Margaret Lloyd in her comparison of Duncan and Wigman: "Isadora moved as a sculptural figure, as it were, self-contained and complete, regardless of physical surroundings. . . Wigman's attitude to the subject was emotional; she felt space as the medium through which she moved in much the same way as the swimmer feels water." Note 89.

Hanya Holm had earlier remarked that "the use of space as an emotional element, an active partner in the dance, is distinctly European. Possibly because of a past more complex and a destiny more at the mercy of outer forces than is the case in America, we have become aware of the dramatic implications in the vision of the individual pitted against the universe. Space, with its constrictions and its immensity, its dark vistas and blinding horizons, becomes for the dancer an invitation or a menace, but in any case, an inescapable element. The American dancer seems frequently to have little use, to be but slightly aware of space except as an incidental factor in design and floor pattern." Note 90.

It is of interest to note that when the German dancer speaks of space, it is always as an emotional and active agent in the dance. Its presence thus implies pain, anguish, despair, conflict. In passing, one might remark on the incidence of these emotional qualities in Greek art during its decline, and on the European artists' obsession with such qualities in the 20th century.

See also GERMAN DANCE, SPACE, HARMONY IN.

SPACE, HARMONY IN. Rudolf von Laban's analysis of form in movement, the changing relation of the dancer to space, has been codified in a series of swings performed within a geometrical form, the icosahedron. The figure eight, a form of continuous movement, has been developed into a series of twelve swings directed toward or from the twelve points of the icosahedron in the vertical, the horizontal, and the lateral planes. "Laban has demonstrated that the most harmonious sequence of these possible movements is not haphazard but follows certain rules which link the sequence of our movements into a scale. This movement-scale uses twelve directions, that is, twelve movements towards the twelve points of the icosahedron, just as a musical octave consists of twelve tones. The great value of the icosahedron may now be realized: it helps dance students to visualize the points from, and toward which, to move. There are two main scales, the masculine and the feminine, corresponding to minor and major in music. Forms of expression, using these scales, permit almost infinite possibilities of variation. In addition, the force (dynamics) of the movements and their rhythm offer further variations. The continuity of movements may be altered in the icosahedron to follow the requirements of timing, dynamics, and space-rhythm, blending together stabile and labile movements." Note 91.

Laban's system has been given the name choreutics. Its purpose is to give the dancer an awareness of space and to give the choreographer a sense of masses flowing in space. Space is here considered as a tangible fluid like water.

SPACE PATTERN. Denotes the lines marked by the body and its members in space. The lines are usually made by the arms and legs since they are the most expressive members of the complete body. Space pattern is to be distinguished from floor pattern which is restricted to the lines marked by the fleet on the floor.

SPEECH PHRASE. A series of connected movements or a movement-rhythm depending upon the breath length; term borrowed from speech because the modern dance consciously uses the breath-rhythm which causes movements as well as spoken words to fall into groups of varying lengths within a larger whole.

Used in conjunction with the kinesthetic phrase, which is the way of moving the body by its physical possibilities: change of weight. The two together constitute what is called a movement-phrase. The speech phrase, with its pauses similar to those of the spoken written phrase or sentence, provides rhythm. Doris Humphrey.

See also MOTOR PHRASE.

SPHERICAL HEIGHT. Term used to indicate a type of movement which, if graphed, would be composed of a series of ripples or undulations. Franziska Boas.

SPINAL STRETCH. Any movement in an exercise which involves a pulling or stretching of the spinal column. It may be an upward pull of the vertical torso but is usually some form of torso bend.

STABILE MOVEMENT. Used particularly by Rudolf von Laban in reference to the six odd-numbered swinging movements in the series of twelve swings he has developed, using the icosahedron as a framework. Stabile movements are strong, quick, or active in character, and generally tight and closed in dimension.

STACCATO. In music, detached; in dance, any movement separated, detached, broken, not flowing.

Antonym: LEGATO.

STATIC TENSION. An inward continual building of tension, although no movement occurs; personal projection through a held position or a held tension. The nerves and the muscles are brought into opposition to each other so that the result is tension that does not result in movement.

See also RESISTANCE, SUSPENSION.

STENOCHOREGRAPHY. A system of signs and symbols devised to record dance or other movements on paper. Preferred term is dance notation.

STEP. Any transfer of weight from one member of the body to another, but is usually restricted to a transfer from one foot to the other. This simple transfer is a primary movement, used as a basis for all variations in space, time, and dynamics, for which see STEP-SCALE. Step is also the basis for fall-recovery which is not included in Hanya Holm's step-scale.

STEP-SCALE. An ordering of transitional movements used by Hanya Holm and based on the step as the primary movement. This primary phase of motion is divided into an active and a passive impulse.

1. The active impulse is that which conditions the step by conscious driving power and momentum. The will to overcome gravity is here clearly marked. Active moments are further divided into three parts: those which stress a horizontal line, those which stress an upward or vertical line, and those which stress a downward line.

a. Horizontal advance: there are three degrees of this advance: the step, the run, and the race.

1) The step which stresses the horizontal advance is a simple, sharp, well-marked step which is produced with more vigor and conscious direction than usual.

2) The run is produced when a more strongly stressed horizontal advance causes a quickening in time.

3) The race is produced when this advance reaches its maximum speed.

b. High advance: there are three degrees of this advance: the step, the leap, and the skip.

1) The step here stresses the upward motion of each transfer of weight and gives buoyancy and elasticity to the movement.

2) The leap occurs when this upward motion is increased to its maximum; it may be said to include an air-moment, and the transfer of weight occurs during that moment.

3) The skip occurs when the downward motion of the step is stressed and also includes an air-moment; but here the transfer of weight occurs after the air-moment.

c. Deep advance: there are two degrees of this advance: the stamp and the lunge.

1) The stamp occurs when the drive is downward and forward and stresses the need of great resistance to the pull of gravity. If the pull of gravity is strong and is accepted, a fall will result which does not belong to the step-scale.

2) The lunge occurs when the power of gravity and momentum is allowed to exert a strong pull and brings the body to the verge of a fall, without allowing the fall to occur.

2. The passive impulse is that in which the will-power and driving force are held in abeyance and the movement seems to occur of its own volition. Such movement has a sustained, floating quality. There are three types of step under this heading: the glide, the float, and the sink.

a. The glide occurs on a horizontal level and is a smooth, sliding step.

b. The float occurs on a horizontal level at a short distance above the ground, or seems so to occur, and gives the body an ethereal quality.

c. The sink combines these two types of step, as: float, glide, and sink; float, glide, and sink; and gives a sinuous rocking effect.

STRAIGHT MOVEMENT. A straight movement is any movement in a single plane which draws a straight line, as, when the arm, bent with the fist against the front shoulder, unbends in a forward direction parallel with the floor. Hanya Holm.

See also BROKEN STRAIGHT.

STRESS. The emphasis upon any movement or group of movements over and above other movements that precede or follow it. Stress may be achieved by a change in the quality of the movement or by greater intensity or greater speed in the movement.

Synonym: ACCENT.

STUDY. An exercise or étude concentrating on a single movement-phrase or motive for the purpose of training the student in the mastery of special difficulties in regard to the manipulation of the body; or, beyond such an executive purpose, to stress quality, mood, emotional feeling, etc.

SUCCESSION. "The emphasis in succession is on flow, on overlapping movement, which may move from one individual to another, from one movement to another, or from one group-segment to another. New movements arise before the preceding ones have reached their termination; new directions are taken before the old direction dies; new rhythms begin in the reverberations of the rhythms before. It is, to a large extent, the succession which gives the dance form. A succession may, likewise, be occasionally stopped on an accent, in which case it becomes a design in space. If the flow has been well stated before the accent-stop is made, it may continue again without loss of connection, provided, of course, that the interval of cessation is not too long. This is the same thing that holds true in music, where too great an interval makes the following rhythm unable to establish its connection." Note 92.

Succession is one of the three divisions in design listed by Doris Humphrey, the other two being opposition and unison.

SUSPENSATORY MOVEMENT. See SUSPENSION.

SUSPENSION. Any movements which are appreciably lengthened in time to give an aerial quality, an isolation, a momentary freedom with gravitational pull to the movement. A breath-expansion is necessary to give the floating quality to the movement.

See also OPPOSITIONAL TENSION, RESISTANCE, SUSTAINED MOVEMENT, TILT.

SUSTAINED CONTROL. Some degree of tension through an entire

dance or exercise. Sustained control refers to those places in a dance or transition to which the term "relaxation" is usually applied. Relaxation, however, infers deadness, inertia, conclusion, and when this happens to movement there is a dead spot in the dance. Sustained control implies movement that is dynamic and living even though less tensed, more relaxed.

SUSTAINED LINE. Any movement-phrase or series of phrases in logical, fluent, sustained, and evenly advancing line.

SUSTAINED MOVEMENT. Any movement whose time-span is purposely lengthened either during its progress or at its peak, this lengthening giving an aerial quality to the movement, emphasizing it, and momentarily isolating it as though it were suspended in mid-air.

See also CONTROLLED MOVEMENT, OPPOSITIONAL TENSION, RESISTANCE, SUSPENSION, TILT.

SWAYING. Similar to a pendular swing, but inverted. In the pendular swing, the point of suspension may be in the pelvis for a leg swing or in the shoulder or upper chest for an arm swing. In swaying, the point of suspension is at the bottom, either in the pelvis or in the lower extremities.

SWING. "Swaying or rocking movement, responding to the pull of gravity. Force is applied in an impetus which is a tipping off balance. The follow-through is in a long arc or curve. Swings may be pendular, circular, or figure-8, or they may combine 2 or more of these forms." Note 93.

Swings have been most carefully analyzed by Rudolf von Laban. See SPACE, HARMONY IN.

SYMPHONIC BALLET. Denotes a ballet composition based upon already-written music, usually a symphony. See MUSIC-VISUALIZATION.

SYMPHONIC FORM. One of the compositional forms in modern dance; a group dance of considerable length, built in abstract, non-representational movement on several themes and their variations. Not to be confused with symphonic ballet, which is a ballet re-expressing a symphony. In a symphonic form, the music is written after the dance has been composed, or during its composition.

SYNCHORIC ORCHESTRA. The name given by Ruth St. Denis to a large group of dancers visualizing a musical work. "The Synchoric Orchestra, when dancing in connection with a Symphony Orchestra to visualize a symphony, would be composed of as many dancers as there were musical instruments. Each dancer would be definitely related to one certain instrument. Some arrangement of human values is desirable; such as the heavier and older dancers paralleling the heavier instruments, strong men for percussion and brass, slender youths for the woodwinds, young girls for violins, and more mature girls and women for 'cellos and basses. Each dancer would move exactly what was played by his instrument and when his instrument was silent he would be still. When all the violins played in unison, all the violin dancers would dance in a unified group, in unison of movement. A solo theme by a flute, against an accompaniment of 'cellos and basses would be seen as a solo dance movement by the flute dancer, with subordinated mass movement in the background upon the part of the dancers representing the 'cellos and bases. The whole would always maintain an architectural sense of mass composition, so that at all times the grouping was based on a sound undertaking of form.

"About six years ago, in 1919 I visualized the two movements of the Unfinished Symphony of Schubert. For months I worked with more than sixty dancers who were all pupils of Denishawn, well-trained and responsive human instruments in my Synchoric Orchestra. For the obvious reason of expense, I was unable to have a symphony orchestra, but with the conductor's score, and the invaluable help of Mr. Louis Horst, our pianist-director, each instrument's scoring was studied, and the movements of that dancer worked out first separately, then in relation to the other instruments of his class, and then in relation to the form of the whole.

". . . The Dalcroze School is a burning and shining light, and probably for that very reason has not made the headway in this country by 1925 that it should, for it demands a mental activity that the average pupil is unable or unwilling to give. I have long said we are still in the main satisfied with the physical plane in dancing, and as long as the Ned Wayburn type satisfies the average theatre-goer, the question of true music-dancing will have to struggle along with its self-appointed pioneering task." Note 94.

This is an extremely mechanical method of dance composition, used in relation to music-visualization. The Synchoric Orchestra, however, is of historical importance because it was one of the first attempts by the modern dance to compose in large terms. Its dependence upon the musical instrument defeated its purpose. The musical instrument performs in terms of sound; when it is silent, its presence is obliterated from the attention of the spectator. The dancer, however, performs in terms of visual images and is unable to obliterate himself when not performing. A dancer remaining motionless for too long a period will increasingly force himself upon the attention of the spectator and become increasingly disturbing.

TECHNIQUE. 1. "The method or the details of procedure essential to expertness of execution in any art, science, etc., hence, manner of performance with reference to such expertness." Note 95.

2. In the dance, any particular exercise or study used to train the student in the mastery of bodily movements.

TEMPO. The rate of speed with which a series of movements is performed. Physical correpondences are found for the following musical terms: hesitatingly for largo, slowly for lento, smoothly for adagio, moderately for andante, briskly for allegro, and hurriedly for presto.

TENSION. 1. The act of stretching or straining, or the state resulting from such action.

2. "To tense means to develop force, to contract or expand two opposites. A bridge is a tension between two pillars. Expanding is the result, from forces outside, of two opposed contractions, as in a rubber band stretched by the fingers. Tension is used in the dance as either muscular or intensity tension. Muscular tension is called contraction, whereas the term 'tension' is reserved for the condition resulting from a contraction, or for the contraction and its result combined. It is a loaded condition, full of energy and power." Hanya Holm.

See also TENSION-RELAXATION.

TENSION-RELAXATION. During the formal development of the modern dance in the 1920's and 1930's, the theory of tension-relaxation was invoked as a major principle. Inasmuch as a dancer was working in sequential movement and the movement iself was the result of muscular action, as John Martin has remarked, it became apparent that the dance and all of its subdivisions were a constant fluctuation between the poles of complete relaxation and complete tension.

Isadora Duncan was aware of this ebb and flow of muscular impulse; however, she was unable to formulate it as a governing principle in her work. Jaques-Dalcroze stated in 1907 that "by means of movements of the whole body, we may equip ourselves to realise and perceive rhythms. This consciousness of rhythm is acquired by means of muscular contractions and relaxations in every degree of strength and rapidity." Note 96. In Germany, Rudolf von Laban stressed particularly this dynamic aspect of movement and, partly through his influence, tension-relaxation (Anspannung und Abspannung) was established as a controlling principle in the work of Mary Wigman in the 1920's.

Tension-relaxation is used mainly in reference to the German dance. Jan Veen (Hans Wiener) has defined it as follows: "Consideration of rhythm leads to the polar principles of relaxation and tension. Complete relaxation is one hundred per cent working of gravity in body function. It is a fiercely conscious faculty in itself far removed from sluggishness. It is a concentration away from activity. But there is a world of difference between unconscious and controlled relaxation. The former spells inertia, the latter means release of energy. At the opposite end of the relaxation-tension pole is tension, which is contraction of muscle, the concentration of force in its most animate form. Tension is an unswerving drive in any direction in defiance of gravity or inertia. When tension is the aim there can be no compromise with softness nor can relaxation be curbed by restraint. Each in its final development is a diametrically straight action. Relaxation is a ninety-degree drop in relation to the ground, and tension is a drive in any given direction." Note 97.

Although frequent efforts have been made to stress the quality of control in the relaxation, it seems nevertheless true that "the German theory works almost completely on a physical-muscular basis; thus, tension becomes strain and indicates a peak of muscular energy; and relaxation, simply through physical limitations, becomes a degree of exhaustion. Balance and unbalance, on the contrary, are the shifting between the poles of immobility; there may be strain and exhaustion, or there may not be. The chief aim is a perpetual balancing between the poles, whereas the Germans are more inclined to carry their efforts to an extreme. They approach the destruction-pole too closely and stay near it too continuously, so that their only possibility finally is to return to the stasis-pole for a longer interval than should be necessary, or to arrive at the destruction pole, which means to fall on the floor." Note 98.

Tension-relaxation as a governing principle results in a highly subjective expressionistic dance. The connotation of inertia or exhaustion which relaxation seems to carry has led the American dancer to avoid the term. For a similar dynamic principle, Martha Graham uses the term "contraction-release," and Doris Humphrey uses the term "fall-recovery." In 1938, Dane Rudhyar attempted to clarify the term. "The two terms 'tension' and 'relaxation' are therefore not to be used in dance as polar opposites. One should say instead: tension and release. Tensions are produced not only by relationships between two polar forces, but also by differences of level, as in waterfalls, or of potential, electrical, and even spiritual psychological energy. I am led to understand that Mary Wigman does not think of abspannung, usually translated as relaxation, as meaning a complete discharge of muscular power leading to a state of collapse or emptiness. It means a controlled release. No creative release should lead to an absolute exhaustion of tension." Author's note: It is interesting in this respect to quote Arthur Michel, German dance critic, on Mary Wigman's Evening Dances which are characteristic of most of the work she has performed in America: "In them, the deeply stirred, sonorous melody of body-movement again and again would cease abruptly. A fierce, sweeping ascent would sink back repeatedly into physical suffocation, weariness, darkness. They ended, on the whole, in collapse or resignation. Such were their most striking characteristics. Note 99 . . ." And it is very interesting to note that while Mary Wigman seems to have emphasized the two first states of the complete cycle of activity in any form, tension and release, Martha Graham stresses the two last ones, fall and recovery." Author's note: This seems to be an error in attribution. It is Doris Humphrey who has developed and expounded upon the principle of fall and recovery." The entire cycle is made up of four great movements or stages of becoming: tension, release, fall and recovery. Tension is the stage preliminary to activity proper. It is, as Hanya Holm said, 'readiness for release.' It is the seed of action. Release is action seen from the point of view of the origin of the action: that which was tensioned is now being released. Fall is . . . action in which the definite awareness of the end of action is contained. . . But the fall does not end and recovery takes place. The body reasserts its will to the vertical, which is the will to the state of creative tension." Note 100.

By limiting tension to a state of readiness for acion, Mr. Rudhyar has removed it from its general meaning in tension-relaxation. The tension in tension-relaxation refers to a series of movement-phrases or periods of increasing tenseness in the dance itself.

TENSION-RELEASE. See under TENSION-RELAXATION.

TEXTURE. Denotes one aspect of style, the other being contour. Texture refers to the inner tensions that exist in all movements used in the modern dance. Term is vague.

See also CONTOUR.

THEMATIC DANCE. Term suggested by Helen Tamiris to replace "abstract dance," in view of the fact that movement in any dance of any type is to some degree abstracted. A thematic dance is one which builds on themes and their variations without recourse to specific subject matter and might be considered similar to pure music as distinguished from programme music. If generally accepted, it would include two terms now generally used: abstract dance and dramatic dance, and its antonym would be pantomimic dance. Some confusion, however, may result because of this, inasmuch as the dance built on abstract movement for the sheer joy of dynamic design, and the dance built on abstract movement to convey an emotional mood or an idea and its ramifications, using dramatic unity, are sufficiently different to merit distinction.

TILT. A variety of fall in which the tensed body tilts usually forward or sideward and then is caught by a thrust of the foot before the fall is completed. It may be likened to a vertical straight line moving toward a horizontal position. Not to be confused with the word "lean" which could be a similar movement by one part of the body, whereas tilt is performed by the whole body kept as long as possible in a straight line. The period of unbalance is prolonged and, being consciously felt, enlivens the transitional phrase between the two points of rest or balance. Helen Tamiris.

May be considered one variety of the quality called suspension inasmuch as the breath is held at expansion and the body appears to be suspended. See also CONTROLLED MOVEMENT, OPPOSITIONAL TENSION, RESISTANCE, SUSTAINED MOVEMENT.

TORSION. The act of twisting or turning; more specifically, a rotation of the spine.

TRANSFER. See CHANGE OF WEIGHT.

TRANSITION. 1. The arc which connects the beginning and end of a movement; stressed by modern dance and usually obliterated by the ballet. The latter reckons with extremities of intervals, eliding the connecting movement to provide a greater aerial quality and thereby working in linear rather than spatial design and removing the natural body rhythms into abstract automatism. Modern dance reckons with the interval in its entirety, utilizing the connecting movement, transition, as well as the extremities of the movement, and thereby working more spatially.

2. Transition is also used to indicate the various foot movements: walk, run, leap, slide, etc. which bridge the gap between various movement-phrases at different points on the stage, or between two static designs, etc.

TURNING. Rotation around an axis, in the same place or in the same plane. Because of the hypnotizing quality of turns, they are likely to be carried to the point of exhaustion, as they were in some of the solo dances of Mary Wigman.

TURNING AXIS. See AXIAL MOVEMENT.

TWISTING. A rotary movement similar to turning but differing from it in that it will use more than one axis and will progress through more than one plane. Twisting will have somewhat the same hypnotizing effect as turning but its duration will be shorter because of the greater instability that it imposes upon the body.

UNACCOMPANIED DANCE. See DANCE WITHOUT MUSIC.

UNFOLDING. See FOLDING-UNFOLDING.

UNISON. One of the three divisions in design, the other two being opposition and succession. Unison is a symmetrical pattern or design for a single figure or group as seen from the spectator's point of view. Illustration: a single erect figure with arms raised to each side at right angles to the body. Doris Humphrey

UP-STROKE. An upward motion used in translating the musical accent. Elizabeth Selden.

See also DOWN-STROKE.

VIBRATION. A small vertical movement repeated many times. Franziska Boas.

WAVE RHYTHM. One of the natural rhythms observed by Isadora Duncan and consciously used by her followers and imitators. "With the strengthening of the breeze over the seas, the waters form in long undulations. Of all movement which gives us delight and satisfies the soul's sense of movement, that of the waves of the sea seems to me the finest. This great wave movement runs through all Nature, for when we look over the waters to the long line of hills on the shore, they seem to have the great undulating movement of the sea; and all movements in Nature seems to me to have as their ground-plan the law of wave movement." Note 101. This statement, written about 1905 by Isadora Duncan, seems to stress an undulating line above all else. Later, in an undated manuscript called Depth, Duncan had arrived at the dynamic principle that was to govern all modern dancing. "The movements," she says, "should follow the rhythm of the waves: the rhythm that rises, penetrates, holding in itself the impulse and the after-movement; call and response, bound endlessly in one cadence." Note 102.

The use of these natural rhythms was later formulated under the term dynamism.

WEIDMAN, CHARLES, THEORY. One of the three dancers emerging from the Denishawn School who established the modern dance in America. Weidman left the Denishawn School in 1928, when, in conjunction with Doris Humphrey, he gave his first New York recital. Terms associated with Weidman are distorted opposition, intensity, kinetic pantomime. Those things listed under the theory of Hanya Holm are directed toward the analysis of movement; those under the theory of Isadora Duncan state the emotional qualities of dynamic movement; those under the theory of Mary Wigman elaborate the subjective, emotional qualities of dynamic movement through physico-muscular means; those under the theory of Doris Humphrey are directed mainly toward composition for groups of dancers; those under the theory of Martha Graham enunciate a dynamic principle and indicate a content on the unconscious or subconscious level; those of Charles Weidman are entirely concerned with the stylization of pantomimic movement.

WIDE. Denotes any movement which is performed with the greatest possible pull, stretch, or extension.

Antonym: NARROW.

WIGMAN, MARY, THEORY. The most important creative dancer in Germany, from whose studio emerged such dancers as Hanya Holm, Yvonne Georgi, Harald Kreutzberg, and Kurt Jooss. After studying with Dalcroze and Rudolf von Laban, her own style matured by 1924. The most important terms associated with her are dance without music, tension-relaxation, expressionistic dance, and space. See also absolute dance, functional movement, German dance, sequential movement, music. Those things listed under the theory of Charles Weidman are entirely concerned with the stylization of pantomimic movement; those under the theory of Hanya Holm are directed toward the analysis of movement; those under the theory of Doris Humphrey are directed mainly toward composition for groups of dancers; those under the theory of Martha Graham enunciate a dynamic principle and indicate a content on the unconscious or subconscious level; those under the theory of Isadora Duncan state the emotional qualities of dynamic movement; those under the theory of Mary Wigman elaborate the subjective, emotional qualities of dynamic movement through physico-muscular means.

# NOTES

1. John Martin, **America Dancing** (Dodge, N.Y., 1936), p. 66.
2. **Webster's Collegiate Dictionary** (Merriam, Springfield, Mass., 1947).
3. Martin, p. 92.
4. John Martin, **The Dance** (Tudor, N.Y. 1946), p. 10.
5. Frederick Rand Rogers, ed., **Dance: A Basic Educational Technique** (Macmillan, N.Y., 1941), p. 72, (Chapter by John Martin).
6. Emile Jaques-Dalcroze, **Rhythm, Music and Education** (Putnam, N.Y., 1921), pp. 280-281.
7. **Grove's Dictionary of Music and Musicians,** 3rd ed., (Macmillan, N.Y., 1947), II, p. 229.
8. Theodore Meyer Greene, **The Arts and the Art of Criticism** (Princeton Univ. Press, Princeton, N.J., 1940), p. 129.
9. Grove, I, p. 548.
10. Isadora Duncan, **The Art of the Dance** (Theatre Arts, N.Y., 1928), pp. 136-137.
11. Duncan, p. 136.
12. Glen Tetley, "**Status of Notation: 'Choroscript'," Dance Observer,** xv, 9, (Nov. 1948), pp. 116-117.
13. Alwin Nikolais, "**Choroscript: A New Method of Dance Notation," Theatre Arts,** xxxii, 2, (Feb. 1948), pp. 63-66.
14. Duncan, p. 100.
15. Duncan, p. 141.
16. Duncan, p. 99.
17. Rogers, pp. 185-186, (Chapter by Martha Graham).
18. Grove, I Ip,. 737.
19. Greene, pp. 149-150.
20. Ann Barzel, "**European Dance Teachers in the United States," Dance Index,** III, 4-5-6 (1944), pp. 71-72.
21. Virginia Stewart, ed., **Modern Dance** (Weyhe, N.Y., 1935), pp. 111-112, (Chapter by Paul Love).
22. Stewart, p. 124, (Chapter by Paul Love).
23. John Martin, "The Dance: Distortion," **N.Y. Times,** date unknown.
24. Duncan, p. 22.
25. Duncan, p. 90.
26. Margaret Lloyd, **The Borzoi Book of Modern Dance** (Knopf, N.Y., 1949), p. 6.
27. Sergei Eisenstein, "The Principles of Film Form," **Experimental Cinema.** Cinema, 4 (1933), pages unknown.
28. Duncan, p. 69.
29. Duncan, p. 19.
30. Duncan, p. 90.
31. Grove, II, p. 767.
32. Jaques-Dalcroze, pp. 81-82.
33. Stewart, p. 31 (Chapter by Harald Kreutzberg).
34. Stewart, p. 19 (Chapter by Mary Wigman).
35. Stewart, pp. 131-132 (Chapter by Hanya Holm).
36. Stewart, p. 132 (Chapter by Hanya Holm).
37. Rogers, pp. 189-190 (Chapter by Doris Humphrey).
38. Grove II, p. 320.
39. Mary Wigman, "**Composition in Pure Movement," Modern Music,** VIII, 2, (1931), p. 20.
40. Stewart, p. 5, (Chapter by Artur Michel).
41. Stewart, pp. 5-6, (Chapter by Artur Michel).
42. Stewart, p. 17, (Chapter by Artur Michel).
43. Stewart, p. 22, (Chapter by Mary Wigman).
44. Stewart, p. 133, (Chapter by Hanya Holm).
45. Stewart, p. 131, (Chapter by Hanya Holm).
46. Stewart, p .7, (Chapter by Artur Michel).
47. Alfred Schlee, "**Expressionism in the Dance,**" Modern Music, VIII, 1, (1931), pp. 13-14.
48. Duncan, p. 139.
49. Rogers, pp. 199-201, (Chapter by Juana de Laban).
50. Stewart, p. 121, (Chapter by Paul Love).
51. Webster
52. Martin, **America Dancing,** pp. 110-118.
53. Duncan, p. 17, (Chapter by Margherita Duncan).
54. Duncan, p. 54.
55. Duncan, p. 34, (Chapter by Shaemas O'-Sheel).
56. Duncan, pp. 51-52.
57. Martin, **America Dancing,** pp. 107, 117.
58. Greene, p. 69.
59. Greene, p. 70.
60. Greene, p. 71.
61. Greene, p. 150, footnote 7.
62. Rogers, pp. 193-194, (Chapter by Juana de Laban).
63. Lloyd, p. 41.
64. Stewart, p. 110 (Chapter by Paul Love).
65. John Martin, **Introduction to the Dance** (Norton, N.Y., 1939), p. 69.
66. Grove, IV, p. 146.
67. Stewart, p. 41, Chapter by Hans Hasting.
68. Martin, **Introduction,** pp. 234-235.
69. Wigman, **Composition,** pp. 20-22.
70. Martin, **America Dancing,** p. 158.
71. Ruth St. Denis, "**Music Visualization," The Denishawn Magazine,** I, 3, 1925.
72. Duncan, p. 79.
73. Greene, p. 68.
74. Lloyd, p. 52.
75. Agnes George de Mille, "**The New Ballerina," Theatre Arts,** (May 1931), p. 429.
76. Rogers, pp. 181-182 (Chapter by Martha Graham).
77. Stewart, p. 97 (Chapter by Paul Love).
78. Louis Horst, "**Modern Forms: Rhythm," Dance Observer** (Dec. 1939), pp. 298-299.
79. Stewart, p. 111 (Chapter by Paul Love).
80. H. W. Fowler, **A Dictionary of Modern English Usage,** (Oxford, London, 1926), p. 504.
81. Jaques-Dalcroze, pp. 79-80.
82. Grove, V, 4, p. 426.
83. Duncan, pp. 55-56.
84. Duncan, p. 91.
85. Duncan, p. 99.
86. Duncan, p. 102.
87. Wigman, **Composition,** p. 20.
88. Martin, **Introduction,** p. 64.
89. Lloyd, p. 12.
90. Stewart, p. 132 (Chapter by Hanya Holm).
91. Rogers, pp. 199-209 (Chapter by Juana de Laban).
92. Stewart, p. 112 (Chapter by Paul Love).
93. Ruth Whitney Jones, **Modern Dance in Education,** Bur. of Publications, N.Y., 1947, p. 83.
94. St. Denis.
95. Webster.
96. Jaques-Dalcroze, pp. 79-80.
97. Rogers, pp. 247-248 (Chapter by Jan Veen).
98. Lloyd, passim.
99. Stewart, p. 7 (Chapter by Artur Michel).
100. Dane Rudhyar, "**Notes on Tension, Release and Relaxation,**" Educational Dance, I, 4 (1938), pp. 4-5.
101. Duncan, p. 68.
102. Duncan, p. 99.